Madame Blavatsky
Mother of the New Age

Michael P. Mau

The Sanctus Germanus Foundation
104-743 Railway Avenue Suite 611
Canmore, AB T1W 0C5
Canada

www.sanctusgermanus.net

©2007-2009 This screenplay is copyright and protected internationally under the Berne Convention. All rights are reserved. Apart from any fair dealing for the purpose of production as permitted under the Canadian Copyright Act of 1985, no part of this publication may be reproduced, stored in a retrieval system, or transmitted, in any form or by any means, electronic, electrical, chemical, mechanical, optical, photocopying, recording or otherwise, without the prior permission of the copyright owner, Michael P. Mau and the Sanctus Germanus Foundation.

ISBN: 978-0-9784835-2-4

INT. TIBETAN TRASHI LHUNPO MONASTERY -- NIGHT

Circa 1868 Cold blistery, snowy night in Tibet. TIBETAN MONK opens door to a blast and sees Helena P. Blavatsky (HPB) in winter military uniform. He slams the door in shock. The banging on the door continues. He hesitates, then Buddhist compassion sets in over the personal fright. He reopens the door and lets the stranger in. He motions the stranger to wait standing.

INT. TIBETAN TRASHI LHUNPO MONASTERY-- HEAD LAMA'S OFFICE. -- NIGHT

TWO LAMAS, draped with red woollen robes to ward off the interior cold, are sitting on a raised platform--a kang-- studying a Buddhist text. The room is plain and lit with a small flickering butter-oil lamp, giving them just enough light to read. Suddenly LAMA 1 looks up.

                    LAMA 1
          Upasika has arrived.

Lama 1 nods to Lama 2 and both stare into the flickering lamp, their eyes in a deep trance. We follow Lama 1's gaze as he and Lama 2 begins to fade out. A loud knock brings us back into focus. HPB stands at the door. She slides through the open door and before our eyes the two Tibetan Lamas transform themselves into a Rajput Prince (Master Morya) and a Kashmiri noble (Master Kuthumi)

                    HPB
                (In a low
                 voice)

          Master! Teacher!

HPB bows with her hands in prayer position and prostrates herself on the floor at the feet of the two Masters.

                    MORYA
          Brave chela! Welcome back. You have traveled far,
          all the way from Russia and Constantinople. We have
          been following your progress.

Kuthumi bends forward and lifts her up from the floor. As HPB stands, both Kuthumi and Morya beam a radiant light around HPB. She lingers in the light and is instantly revived.

                              MORYA (CONT'D)
                    You must rest. Your sleeping quarters are next to the
                    monastery. The rest of the monks will not understand
                    that you are really one of us, because you have
                    reincarnated as a woman this time...

                              HPB
                    Not all are ready to see past lives. It doesn't
                    matter. I go where you tell me.

                              MORYA
                    Rest for now. We begin tomorrow.

EXT. TIBETAN TRASHI LHUMPO MONASTERY--ROOFTOP OF ADJOINING
BUILDING- BRIGHT BLINDING SUN... NEXT DAY

HPB is gazing out into the magnificent Himalayas.

The Masters Kuthumi and Morya suddenly appear on the rooftop next
her. All three are facing the mountains

                              KUTHUMI
                    Majestic, aren't they? Look deep into those
                    magnificent Himalayas and you will see the context of
                    your mission.

At first we are drawn into the depth of the calm wondrous
mountains.

Then we see the Master Kuthumi holding a ten-inch diameter brass
Tibetan prayer bowl in his left palm as if he is present an
offering to the mountains. With a carved wooden stick in his
right hand, he strikes the prayer bowl several times. The finely
tuned brass bowl reverberates loudly, sending out several waves of
vibrations that pierce the quiet of the mountains and echo back.

Suddenly, a TEMPEST gathers in the distance. It does not touch
the threesome; rather it takes place like a movie with the
mountains as a backdrop. They peer into the storm and see a
succession of world events: World War I, the 1929 Great
Depression, World War II, the Nazi concentration camps, the
Hiroshima A-Bomb, the Korean War, the Vietnam War, the technology
boom, banks crumbling, Wall Street crash, massive floods, sinking
cities etc. all flashed to them at incredible speed until some
time in the distant future. At that point there is a Christ-like
figure standing in front of the population of the world who calms
the whole tumult. Everyone is covered with bright, almost
blinding light, and the scene unfolds into modern, yet bucolic
cities, farms, and happy people.

KUTHUMI (CONT'D)
Astrologically speaking we have begun to transit out of the Piscean Age into the New Age of Aquarius. This transition happens every 26,000 years more or less. And in every such transition it is necessary to clean out all of mankind's inventions and foibles that do not serve humanity. We keep that which is good. The cleansing process will be tumultuous and is what you just viewed in the tempest. Humanity must pay its karmic debts and right every wrong it has invented.

MORYA
Before this lifetime, you agreed to help us illuminate the Western world with certain concepts, known by the Tibetan Buddhists, that would prepare mankind for this tumult. Your mission will not be easy, for you will collide with mental patterns that have crystallized over centuries and will resist change.

HPB
My memory veil is only just lifting. Please remind me.

KUTHUMI
First, you must show this sceptical world that We, the Trans-Himalayan Brotherhood, exist and are part of an internal Spiritual Hierarchy that governs this earth and its inhabitants. This basic truth has been obscured over the ages.

HPB
But how will I convince them?

KUTHUMI
You will capture their attention through logic and reason backed by manifesting phenomena. You can explain how the phenomena relate to our inner world, which is so close, yet so far from their thinking. The phenomena are meant to capture their attention.

MORYA
Most important is that through reason and spiritual concepts conveyed from your pen, humanity will come to know that all religions come from one root source--the teachings of the Ancient Wisdom--which produce your phenomena and which can help mankind transit into the New Age with less suffering. They must learn that Jesus, Mohammed, Confucius, Buddha, and so many more are brothers sent by us in the Spiritual Hierarchy to teach and open the eyes of mankind. Therefore, there is unity behind all seeming differences in worldly religious ideas. You must demonstrate this fact.

HPB
Why should they listen to me?

KUTHUMI
We are experimenters. We never know what mankind's freewill will return. Some of our own brothers in the Hierarchy remain sceptical, but we are nevertheless willing to expose ourselves to mankind and face their ridicule, stubbornness and slander.

MORYA
Perhaps humanity will mock us as they have done to so many of our messengers. Perhaps they will even attack you. And even worse, they might outwardly agree with you, but not understand anything, and thus betray you. Breaking down ignorance is tougher than storming a fortress. But if this experiment works, the birth of the new age will be rendered less traumatic and the transition can occur in better balance. We will let them choose. We can only give them a choice, which is your true mission.

HPB
Let them mock me. Let them attack me. But if the truth be heard, then I am willing to state it.

KUTHUMI
Will western civilization, which is so proud of its science, see that there is essentially no difference between Science and Religion? This task is more difficult than moving these great Himalayas.

MORYA
If mankind learns that our brothers posed as the great philosophers and scientists who gave civilization science and religion, then mankind might understand.

                    KUTHUMI
          So, Upasika, we give you this last chance to decide if
          you want to carry out this mission.

                    HPB
          There is no doubt in my mind, Master, that I will
          pursue this mission.

SOUND: we hear the ringing of the Tibetan prayer bowl leading us to the change of scene.

                                                  CUT TO:

INT. ODESSA, RUSSIA HOME OF HPB'S AUNT, NADYEZHDA ANDREEVNA FADEEV NOVEMBER 11, 1870 -- MORNING

On screen "Two years later"

NADYEZHDA ANDREEVNA FADEEVA, a short aristocratic Russian woman and HPB's aunt, and her DAUGHTER are seated around the breakfast table. A SERVANT hovers about the breakfast table richly set in the style of Russian aristocracy, pouring tea into empty porcelain cups.

                    NADYEZHDA
               (Handkerchief in hand and sniffling)
          I had a nightmare last night about Lelinka. We've
          heard nothing from her for over two years! All our
          research has come to nothing. Maybe she's imprisoned
          somewhere. She could be dead. She could be dead.
          Where has she gone this time! Canada again? Back to
          Mexico? South America? She will be the end of me.

She throws down her handkerchief on the table, then picks it up and blows into it sniffling.

                    NADYEZHDA (CONT'D)
          My dead sister will never forgive me. I promised to
          watch over her daughter before she passed on. But
          Lelinka just took off one night like that. Like a
          wild beast, wondering the earth. Shooting the papists
          with Garibaldi. With no shame she shows her bullet
          and stab wounds to everyone. What lady would do that?

                    NADYEZDA'S DAUGHTER
          You and aunty made her get married to that disgusting
          old Niki Blavatsky. If I were in her shoes, I would
          run to the other side of the earth, too, and never
          come back!

                    NADYEZHDA
We made a big mistake. She doesn't have to go back to
him. Anyway, she ran away before they could become
man and wife. I wonder if she's still a vir. . . .
All I wish is to see her alive. She can come live
with us. AHHH! She should have been a man. Then we
wouldn't have to worry.

An agitated SERVANT approaches the table.

                    SERVANT
Madame, come quick!

                    NADYEZHDA
What is it?

                    SERVANT
There's a strange ASIAN MAN at the door. He wants to
talk to you. He spoke your name.

NADHEZHDA moves briskly toward the door.

INT: ODESSA, RUSSIA HOME OF HPB'S AUNT-- MAIN DOORWAY--DAY

A dark skinned Asian man stands waiting. He hands her an
envelope, but says nothing. Nadyezhda rips open the envelope and
reads the letter aloud in French.

                    KUTHUMI (V.O.)
**A l'Honorable, Très Honorable Dame, Nadyejda Andreewna
Fadeew**, Odessa.

Les nobles parents de Madame H. Blavatsky n'ont aucune
cause de se désoler. Leur fille et nièce n'a point
quitté ce monde. Elle vit et désire faire savoir a
ceux qu'elle aime, qu'elle se porte bien et se sent
fort heureuse dans la retraite lointaine et inconnue
qu'elle s'est choisie. Elle a été bien malade, mais,
ne l'est plus: car grâce à la protection du Seigneur
Sangyas elle a trouvé des amis devoués qui en prennent
soin physiquement et spirituellement. Que les dames
de sa maison se tranquillisent donc. Avant que 18
lunes nouvelles se lèvent--elle sera revenue dans sa
famille.

                    NADYEZHDA
            (looking relieved and up from the letter and
             whispers to herself)

        Lelinka's still alive. She's still alive! But where
        is she. On the other side of the world. Who wrote
        this letter? Where is that strange man?

She beckons her servant.

                    NADYEZHDA (CONT'D)
        Run! Get him. I want to talk to him.

                    SERVANT
        He's gone, Madame. Disappeared like that, before my
        eyes. Poof! While you were reading the letter.

She snaps her finger to show how the Asian man just disappeared in a flash.

                    NADYEZHDA
            (Holding the letter close to her breast)
        But Lelinka is still alive! My Lord Jesus, please take
        care of her and guide her back to us!

SOUND: we hear the reverberations of the Tibetan prayer bowl leading us to the change of scene.

EXT. CHITTENDAM, VERMONT THE EDDY'S FARM -- LATE AFTERNOON

INSERT: Six years later (1874) . . .

A brilliant sunny Indian summer day in the Vermont countryside that makes even the gloomy old farmhouse look cheerful. Lovely landscape in valley bounded by grassy slopes and rise into mountains covered with gold and crimson leafy groves. A group of people have gathered to observe WILLIAM EDDY, chief medium of the Eddy family produce psychic phenomena and phantoms. We hear someone clanging a caste iron skillet and everybody moves into the farmhouse.

INT. EDDY FARMHOUSE -- LATE AFTERNOON

The Eddy family has prepared dinner for the attendees of tonight's seance, not out of largess for the visitors, but to take advantage of the group's presence to make more money. Eddy's wife CLARA comes around to collect money for the food.

                    CLARA EDDY
          Com'on anty up. This ain't no free meal. Ya wanna
          eat, you pay. Com'on give a few. Five cents. Yaw
          ain't gonna see nothin' like this before in yore life.

We see HPB sitting at the bench table with a French Canadian lady MONIQUE conversing in French. HPB wears a scarlet Garibaldian shirt, hair is a thick blond mop like fleece of a Cotswold ewe and worn shorter than shoulders. Her massive Calmuck face expresses power, culture, imperiousness.

                    CLARA EDDY (CONT'D)
          Com'on ladies. Pay for the meal before you eat. Ya
          cain't eat if ya don't pay.

HPB pulls out a dollar piece from her purse.

                    MONIQUE
          That is too much, Helena!

Ignoring her friend's comment, HPB drops the silver dollar into the pot.

                    CLARA EDDY
          Thank you, ma'am! We gonna give you extra for that,
          ma'am! Much grateful. Wait 'til you see them ghosts.
          Them's real as life.

HPB nods and smiles. Clara puts two plates of food before the two ladies.

ANGLE ON DINNER TABLE HPB'S POV

HPB spots a bespectacled gentleman with a beard, early forties, who enters the farmhouse and approaches the table. She smiles knowingly to herself but continues to converse with her friend in French. COLONEL HENRY S. OLCOTT takes a seat directly opposite them. HPB pretends to ignore him and continues to converse with her friend, knowing the gentleman is eavesdropping on their conversation.

ANGLE ON CLARA EDDY

                    CLARA EDDY (CONT'D)
          Wait a minute there, sir. Didya pay yet?

COLONEL OLCOTT fumbles in his coat pocket and pulls out a coin and gives it to Clara who waves to a man to give Olcott a plate of food.

EXT. EDDY FARMHOUSE GROUNDS -- A SHORT TIME LATER

The two ladies get step outside to breathe in the fresh autumn air after dinner. HPB rolls herself a cigarette.

Olcott steps outside after them and joins the two ladies

              COLONEL OLCOTT
Permettez-moi, madame.

He pulls out some matches and lights HPB's cigarette.

             COLONEL OLCOTT (CONT'D)
What brings you here, ma'm?

             HPB
I'm very interested in these kinds of strange things.

             MONIQUE
She's come to see "fantÙmes", as we call them in French.

             HPB
I read about them in letters sent to the Daily Graphic by a certain Colonel Olcott.

             MONIQUE
This place is so close to Montreal that I came to see them, too.

            COLONEL OLCOTT
  (turning to HPB)
Then you must be from New York.

             HPB
Among other places, yes.

            COLONEL OLCOTT
How long have you been here?

             HPB
I came in on the evening train yesterday and met my friend Monique. And you?

            COLONEL OLCOTT
Several weeks.

                    HPB
          To tell you the truth, I hesitated before coming here
          because I was afraid of meeting that Colonel Olcott.
          Odd fellow. To be so obsessed with these ghostly
          things.

                    COLONEL OLCOTT
          Why should you be afraid of him, Madame?

                    HPB
          Oh! Because I fear he might write about me in his
          paper.

                    COLONEL OLCOTT
          Rest assured, Madame, Mr. Olcott would not mention you
          unless you wished it.

                    HPB
          How would you know, sir?

                    COLONEL OLCOTT
          Because you're speaking to him. Henry Steel Olcott is
          the name. Most call me Colonel Olcott.

Colonel Olcott gives a deep bow but shows absolutely no embarrassment.

                    COLONEL OLCOTT (CONT'D)
               (Offering his arm)
          I hope you don't find this too forward, but shall we
          take a walk through these beautiful colors?

                    MONIQUE
          Excuse me, Monsieur. Helena, I'll leave you two until
          the seance.

She walks away in the opposite direction as HPB and Colonel Olcott.

WIDER ANGLE The two stroll together through the meadow chatting like old friends, leaving behind HPB's French Canadian friend.

                    HPB
          Do you plan to stay for the séance tonight?

                    COLONEL OLCOTT
          Yes, that's why I came. And you?

                  HPB
Yes, it'll be interesting to see how these Americans do it. I've been to quite of few of these in Europe. What have you seen in these séances?

                COLONEL OLCOTT
So far, Red Indians and relatives of the Americans or Europeans attending the séance show up. They take form out of the ectoplasm the medium produces.

                  HPB
Are they genuine? Do they say who they are?

                COLONEL OLCOTT
Oh, they're real spooks, alright. You can see through them. Voices come out of a trumpet. Some will tell you who they are but most don't have any names.

                  HPB
I hope tonight's séance will be more interesting. I haven't come all the way up from New York just to see some spooks mumble nonsense.

                COLONEL OLCOTT
I hope you're not too disappointed. You implied you've been to many places beside New York.

                  HPB
Yes. I've been around the world twice. Canada, out west in America, Mexico, Europe, Egypt, India and . . . Tibet.

                COLONEL OLCOTT
I've only traveled to Europe. But Tibet? So high and so far. How did you manage?

                  HPB
I tried twice. First time the British border guards stopped me. Second time, I dressed up like a man, and they let me through.

COLONEL OLCOTT laughs out loud steps back a bit to get a better look of HPB.

                COLONEL OLCOTT
May I be so presumptuous to ask what did you do in Tibet? I've always been fascinated by that place. How long did you stay?

HPB stares into space as she considers the question. Her eyes glaze over and she stares dreamily into the sky, losing track of time. We see flashes of her standing on the rooftop with the Masters Morya and Kuthumi. They nod to her knowingly. She returns to the conversation.

>   HPB
>   (Changing the subject)
>   I also fought with Garibaldi in the battle of Mentana.
>   Here, look. This is where my left arm was broken in a
>   sabre fight. And here, feel this. This is where a
>   bullet is lodged.

She places Olcott's hand on the back of her shoulder.

>   COLONEL OLCOTT
>   Humm! I can feel it. There's a hole.

>   HPB
>   And there's another bullet in my leg.

HPB bends down and lifts her skirt to show the exact spot on her leg.

Olcott, a bit embarrassed, looks around to see if others are watching them. Then HPB lifts up her blouse part way to show him a scar . . . Olcott looks very embarrassed.

>   HPB (CONT'D)
>   This is where I was stabbed by a stiletto. Right below
>   the heart.

>   COLONEL OLCOTT
>   Incredible. Very interesting life you've led. I feel
>   like an innocent compared to you, but I also fought in
>   the Civil War here in the states.

>   HPB
>   Is that why they call you Colonel?

>   COLONEL OLCOTT
>   Yes! I was a signals officer until I got malaria. Not
>   too exciting. Later the government called on me to
>   head the commission investigating President Lincoln's
>   assassination. But enough about me. What about Tibet?
>   I am fascinated by Tibet. And Egypt. Tell me more.

HPB
Later, my friend. I'll have much time in the future to tell you about these wonderful places. But tell me more about yourself. Do you have a wife?

COLONEL OLCOTT
Yes, Mary is her name.

HPB
Children?

COLONEL OLCOTT
Two sons, age 12 and 14. Yes, I think the elder should have turned 14 by now. Fine sons.

HPB
What does your wife think of your interest in these seances?

COLONEL OLCOTT
She'll have nothing to do with them. Strict Presbyterian clergyman's daughter.

HPB
Is she inclined to let you stay away for several weeks at a time to write about spooks?

COLONEL OLCOTT
(Laughing)
She has nothing to say about what I do with my time. Besides, she thinks I'm covering the big railroad scandal in upstate New York.

HPB
But she'll read those articles you write.

COLONEL OLCOTT
Never! She won't even touch the paper they've been printed on! But my life is so boring. Tell me more about your travels

HPB
(Seeming momentarily distracted)
Shouldn't we start back to attend the séance?

COLONEL OLCOTT
Yes, I think his wife is clanging again on the big pot. That means séance is about to begin.

HPB laughs out loud.

                    COLONEL OLCOTT (CONT'D)
          May I contact you when I get back to New York? I
          believe you have many experiences in far away countries
          that my readers would like to know more about.

We hear the clanging of Mrs. Eddy's pot in the background.

                    HPB
          Certainly. We'd better hurry.

                    COLONEL OLCOTT
          Now, let's see what the Eddy's have in store for us.

                                                  CUT TO:

INT. BACK AT THE EDDY FARMHOUSE -- EVENING

FADE IN to an ongoing séance. A candle burns on a small wooden table placed outside a curtained cabinet that has been set up against the wall. Visitors sit on three rows of benches facing the cabinet. The audience can hear WILLIAM EDDY, the medium, inside the cabinet breathing heavily and making strange noises. Suddenly with gasps arising from the audience, a small white trail of smoke emerges from the crack in the cabinet. It jettisons out to the front of the room, building in size and form until it creates the essence of a YOUNG BOY who is transparently visible in the ectoplasm. His voice springs forward out of the white filmy substance.

                    YOUNG BOY
          My master beat me. He killed me in Georgia. That's
          how . . .

Before he could finish, the ectoplasm transforms into an older, traditionally dressed Muslim man, and the young boy fades out

                    MUSLIM MAN
          I am a Muslim merchant from Tiflis. I'm not dead as
          you can see. I'm here to talk to you about . . .

Before he could go on, a KURDISH CAVALIER armed with pistols and a lance comes through. There's a muffled scream from one of the séance sitters.

Then a devilish looking AFRICAN SORCERER wearing a coronet with four horns of onyx and some bells emerges from the ectoplasm. More muffled screams and moans from the sitters.

A EUROPEAN GENTLEMAN wearing the cross and collar of St. Anne

                    HPB
               (Whispering to Olcott)
          That one is my dead uncle. He can't talk because
          that's just an astral shell of him. His soul's already
          moved on to higher places.

                    COLONEL OLCOTT
          So these spooks are not real?

                    HPB
          Some are just souless shells of the former people, like
          my uncle. But those who talk are astral shells with
          souls that still have not evolved higher.

The séance ends and Clara rushes up to doorway with her kitchen pot.

                    CLARA EDDY
          A good show, weren't it? Give up a couple more. Ya
          can afford it. Here, just drop it intah mah pot.

                    HPB
          Ah! Money. This seems to be the state of these
          seances. It's all about making money. Nothing much
          spiritual about it all.

                    COLONEL OLCOTT
          It's like a show. This has been the most interesting
          array of spooks I've seen since I came here. As you
          can see, this poor illiterate Eddy has no idea what
          he's bringing through--people from lands he doesn't
          even know exist. But you recognized them right away,
          didn't you?

                    HPB
          I did indeed. They came from my region of the world.
          Well, Colonel Olcott,
               (changing the subject abruptly)
          This has been quite an extraordinary day and a séance
          well worth my trip up here. By the time you return to
          New York in a month or so, I shall be staying in
          Philadelphia. Please call on me there. I will write
          you at the Daily Graphic with my Philadelphia address.
          I have much to tell you.

SOUND: we hear the ringing of the Tibetan prayer bowl leading us
to the change of scene.

                                             CUT TO:

INT. HPB'S HOME IN PHILADELPHIA--LIVING ROOM -- WINTER DAY

INSERT: Two months later . . .

Typical Philadelphia brick rowhouse on a shaded street.

Colonel Olcott is standing near the fireplace warming his hands by the fire. HPB is seated in a large, comfortable sofa chair.

COLONEL OLCOTT
I brought this reporter's notebook with me so I could take accurate notes. Much of what I'm learning seems so familiar but I feel I must note more details down.

Olcott pulls out the notebook from his coat pocket and shows it to HPB. She closes her eyes for a second. We see a Rosicrucian symbol flash out, a ball of light engulfs it and shoots down into the notebook in Olcott's hand.

HPB
Open it up.

Olcott opens the notebook.

COLONEL OLCOTT
What is this? It was blank a few minutes ago when I bought it. There's now a drawing of a Rosicrucian jewelled crown with the word "fate" written over it and your name "Helena" under it. How did you do that?

HPB
I merely pictured the drawing in my mind and some elementals helped me embed it in your notebook.

COLONEL OLCOTT
Elementals? You confuse me more, Helena.

HPB
Yes. They are little fairy-like entities which we can all learn to control one of these days to help us do wonderful things. One day. This will be known to you. Let's have some tea.

Olcott, still a bit bewildered, sits down next to the tea table, and HPB pours a cup of tea.

HPB (CONT'D)
Here, Henry, have some milk . . . the way you like it.

COLONEL OLCOTT
There was an article about you in the Daily Graphic. Part of a series on Russian émigrés. . .

HPB
Oh! That must have been that reporter who came to see me while I was working at Mr. Levi's factory. I was destitute when I arrived in New York. And what money my father left me I squandered in an ill-fated investment with some other Russian emigres.

COLONEL OLCOTT
That's what the article said. Also, it said you traded in your First Class passage on the ship so that you could help a lady and her children who had been cheated by some ticket vendor.

HPB
Yes. I saw her weeping on the side of the road. They wouldn't let her on the ship because her ticket was a fake and she didn't have a cent. I only had my ticket, so I cashed it in and we had enough for everyone.

COLONEL OLCOTT
Then you must have crossed the Atlantic in steerage.

HPB
It wasn't all that unpleasant but we all got here without a scratch.

Suddenly, there is a rapping sound.

COLONEL OLCOTT
What's that?

HPB
That's an elemental wanting to communicate something to you. Do you know the Morse Code?

COLONEL OLCOTT
Why yes. Remember, I was a signals officer in the army.

HPB
Good. Listen to the raps and take down the message.

The raps sound out from above the tea table, and Olcott diligently takes down the message.

> COLONEL OLCOTT
> It says this is a message from John King. He asks if I like the emblem he embedded in my new notebook. Wait more coming . . .

More raps come through.

> COLONEL OLCOTT (CONT'D)
> It says, the Master from Egypt, from the Brotherhood of Luxor will now take charge of my occult training. He is called the Master Serapis Bey.

> HPB
> He and others of the Brotherhood of Luxor trained me as well while I was in Egypt.

More raps. Olcott takes down the Morse code.

> COLONEL OLCOTT
> The Master will work with me every night. I am to be prepared with all the readings he gives me the previous night.

> HPB
> So they have accepted you.

> COLONEL OLCOTT
> Yes, but who are these Masters?

> HPB
> I call them Mahatmas or great souls. They are living men, not "spirits" who have evolved further along in human evolution. Their knowledge and learning are immense, and their personal holiness of life is still greater.

> COLONEL OLCOTT
> But why do they bother with us?

> HPB
> They have boundless compassion for us still struggling with the problems of human evolution, so they forego their final liberation in order to remain close to humanity and help it move forward.

> COLONEL OLCOTT
> They must be very old, then.

                    HPB
That I cannot say. Hundreds of years old perhaps but
not thousands. All I know is that every time I meet
Master Morya he appears in his prime of manhood while I
seem to get older.

                    COLONEL OLCOTT
I am honored that they see fit to train me. But for
what?

                    HPB
To be my partner in this mission.

                    COLONEL OLCOTT
Your partner? I would like to accept without
hesitation, but I know not what is ahead of me. What
mission?

                    HPB
If you work for the Brotherhood, you only have to know
what is two inches in front of you. Don't fret about
the future. Whatever happens is part of the divine
plan you worked out, so it can't be far from what you
would accept.

                    COLONEL OLCOTT
What if they ask me to leave New York?

                    HPB
Why do you ask?

                    COLONEL OLCOTT
You seem to move around the world for the Masters.

                    HPB
I do according to what they ask me to do. For
instance, what if they were to ask you to move to
India?

Colonel Olcott almost chokes on his tea and puts the cup and saucer down on the table.

COLONEL OLCOTT
Hmmm. What about my wife and two sons? And my law firm. We've just landed some of our biggest clients up to now--The New York Stock Exchange, Mutual Equitable Life and Continental Life, the United Steel Manufactuers of Sheffield England . . . These are big clients we've worked years to get. They pay the bills--my sons' education-- while I investigate spooks as a hobby.

HPB
I just asked. It's something to think about.

They both sit in silence for a second to absorb what has been said. Then Olcott jumps to his feet smiling.

COLONEL OLCOTT
I forgot. I bought these towels from a street vendor at the train station . . . for use around the house.

HPB
How thoughtful of you, Henry! They're nice and soft. I can use them to dust off this furniture.

She takes one and starts to wipe the tea table.

COLONEL OLCOTT
Wait. Shouldn't you hem them first? Isn't that the proper thing to do?

HPB
Oh, Henry, you're so proper. And like the proper lady I was trained to be, I have this sewing basket next to me.

She opens the sewing basket and begins to thread a needle.

HPB (CONT'D)
(Kicking something under the table)

Ouch! Get out of here!

COLONEL OLCOTT
What is it?

HPB
Oh, it's just another elemental who has nothing to do. He wants to help.

COLONEL OLCOTT
Do what?

HPB
Why don't we get it to hem the towels?

COLONEL OLCOTT
But it's an elemental. How could it wield a needle and thread?

HPB
I'll just tell it to do it?

COLONEL OLCOTT
Is it an intelligent creature?

HPB
Sure. But only for specific tasks. Don't ask it to analyze anything. Just tell it to do something specific and it will.

COLONEL OLCOTT
Good test! Let him do the hemming. I'll write an article for the Daily Graphics on this. They'll love it.

HPB
Put this whole bundle of towels in that book cabinet over there.

HPB points to a cabinet then closes her eyes for a second to concentrate. Olcott places the bundle of towels securely in the book cabinet, locks the cabinet door and pops the key into his pocket.

COLONEL OLCOTT
(laughing)
I'll keep them locked up so no one can get in and spoil this experiment. Let our little friends earn their keep. . .

We see HPB close her eyes for a second to concentrate. We see a cluster of scintillating sparkler-like light pierce through the cabinet door to attack the bundle of towels.

COLONEL OLCOTT (CONT'D)
To tell you the truth, I feel like I've been walking in a dream since I met you. Strange things that defy any explanation happen, not only in a seance room but here in this very living room. My mind still has not grasped their real importance, and frankly I sometimes wonder if this isn't a circus act.

HPB
In the hands of the wrong people, this could look like a circus act, but in the hands of the Master Jesus, for instance, he fed thousands.

COLONEL OLCOTT
Then this ability comes from Christianity?

HPB
Absolutely not. The Master Jesus drew this ability from the Ancient Wisdom--cosmic laws. These laws basically go beyond the limitations of scientific laws and church dogma and are the basis of both science and religions. They simply reaffirm man's dominion over matter. This is the key, Henry.

COLONEL OLCOTT
But if this knowledge gets into the hands of the immoral, then what?

HPB
Then you have black magic, sometimes seen in a circus, but mainly in the selfish accumulation of money and power!

COLONEL OLCOTT
Then it is dangerous in the wrong hands.

HPB
Yes, which is why the mastery of basic morals and harmlessness will be so important as we enter the New Age.

COLONEL OLCOTT
Can I one day learn to manifest phenomenon?

HPB
Yes, but you must ask yourself why. Is it to boost personal pride and ambition or do you want this ability to serve humanity. If it's the latter, then you are ready.

                    COLONEL OLCOTT
          I frankly don't know yet.

                    HPB
          Oh! Before I forget. I'm giving a lecture tonight in
          the parlor. Are you interested in attending?

                    COLONEL OLCOTT
          Of course. What's the subject?

                    HPB
          Reincarnation. The Masters want me to release this
          information to the West slowly.

                    COLONEL OLCOTT
          That ought to stir up the ole pot.

Both laugh wickedly.

                                        FADE OUT:

INT. HPB'S HOME IN PHILADELPHIA--LIVING ROOM LATER THAT EVENING

HPB standing in front of a group gathered in her living room.

                    HPB
          So when your physical body dies, your soul, the God
          within, separates from it and travels to a place called
          kamaloka to wait for a new body in which to
          reincarnate. This happens thousands of times as the
          soul comes in and out of lifetimes. It's like changing
          clothes for each different lifetime. With each
          lifetime the soul evolves to higher and higher states
          of consciousness.

                    MAN IN GROUP
          But ma'm, the bible tells us we either go to heaven or
          hell when we die. So we've got one chance to do it.
          Right?

                    HPB
          This is not true. Even in the bible, which is riddled
          with many inaccuracies, there is talk of reincarnation.
          For example, John the Baptist is said to be the
          reincarnation of Elias.

                    WOMAN IN GROUP
          That is blasphemy to talk about the bible like that,
          ma'm. You mean to say we come back in another body?

                        HPB
          Why yes. Some eastern religions even say you might
          come back as an insect if you live an immoral life.
          But in truth, this is not right. You will usually come
          back one notch higher on your evolutionary path unless
          you've been very bad during a particular lifetime.
          Every lifetime is meant to advance you spiritually by
          the lessons you learn on earth. So you could never
          come back as a dog or cat, for instance.

                        MAN IN GROUP
          How about a nigger?

                        HPB
          Of course. Or a Negro woman. Who knows what body your
          soul will choose for the next lifetime in order to
          learn certain lessons?

The group gasps.

                        WOMAN IN GROUP
          God forbid! A nigger man! I've never heard of such a
          thing. Our pastor would die if he heard such!. I
          cannot stay here any longer and listen to this
          blasphemy.

She gathers up her things to leave.

                        HPB
          And you, sir, might come back as a Hindu woman in
          India.

                        MAN IN GROUP
          Damnation! I cannot listen to this woman any longer.
          I must go, too.

The man and woman both get up and stalk out, followed by the
others. The room empties. HPB settles into a chair.

                        HPB
               (Chuckling)
          It went better than I thought.

                        COLONEL OLCOTT
               (chuckling along)
          Did you have to push them that far?

                        HPB
          By god, yes. They'll never forget that lecture on
          reincarnation!

FADE OUT:

INT. LOTUS CLUB RECEPTION NEW YORK -- EVENING

> RECEPTION CLERK
> Welcome back, colonel. Haven't seen you for a few days.

> COLONEL OLCOTT
> I was on business in Philadelphia.

> RECEPTION CLERK
> Here's your mail and your key.

INT. LOTUS CLUB ROOM -- EVENING

Olcott sits at a simple wooden table writing. Suddenly he's aware of a presence. He looks up and sees the vague figure of the Master Serapis Bey, dressed in Egyptian clothes. We see his figure fading in and out although his voice is steady. Olcott immediately stands up and exchanges the Brotherhood salute, Heart, Head and Hand.

> MASTER SERAPIS BEY
> We have impressed further teachings upon your mind that you might consider. Do you have any questions?

> COLONEL OLCOTT
> I do. What is my connection with Helena Blavatsky?

> MASTER SERAPIS BEY
> Your meeting him is not an accident. This is part of a plan we elaborated generations ago when the earth entered into its transition into the New Age. It is an ancient pact that you both have manifested over several lifetimes.

> COLONEL OLCOTT
> I see. So we are meant to work together.

> MASTER SERAPIS BEY
> Yes, this is why she is devoting so much time and effort to elaborate the teachings I've impressed on you.

> COLONEL OLCOTT
> Then I shall do my best to fulfill this plan.

The Master smiles slightly. The Master signals his departure with the salute of the Brotherhood Heart, Head and Hand. Olcott returns the salute.

                                                FADE OUT:

EXT. HPB'S HOME IN PHILADELPHIA -- AFTERNOON

INSERT on screen: "Several weeks later. . ."

Olcott hurries down the street to HPB's rowhouse. He climbs the
stairs and knocks on the door.

HPB's DOMESTIC opens the door.

                    COLONEL OLCOTT
          Will you tell Mme. Blavatsky that Colonel Olcott is
          back from New York?

                    DOMESTIC
          She's gone down aways to get married.

                    COLONEL OLCOTT
          What? You mean she's attending someone's marriage.

                    DOMESTIC
          No, suh, no. She's ah gettin' married herself!

                    COLONEL OLCOTT
          Not possible! You must be wrong.

                    DOMESTIC
          Come in. Dey should be back in 'bout an hour. I'm
          preparin' a little reception for her and her students.

Olcott staggers backward in a state of shock and staggers off.

                                                FADE OUT:

INT. HPB'S HOME IN PHILADELPHIA--LIVING ROOM -- DAY

A few days later . . .

                    HPB
          The maid said you dropped by the other day. You've
          been in Philadelphia for a couple days already? So why
          didn't you call on me earlier?

                    COLONEL OLCOTT
          I was told you got married, so I didn't want to disturb
          you on your honeymoon.

HPB
Don't be silly. It's not anything like what you think. A whim at most. A karmic thing I owed him. His name is Senor Betanelly. You met him a month ago during that discussion we had on Spiritualism. He's infatuated with my mind.

COLONEL OLCOTT
You must be OUT of your mind? He's so much younger than you. And you are, well, so much more, . . . his intellectual superior.

HPB
Ah! Yes. I did it because he promised not to make any demands on me in the wifely sense. And he hasn't. I have my complete freedom to do what I want.

COLONEL OLCOTT
You did before you married him!

HPB
Yes, but you don't understand. He begged and begged me until one day last week I broke down and said yes. And we were married like that! It's karmic, my chum.

COLONEL OLCOTT
Complete foolishness, you mean.

HPB
Come. Come, Henry.

COLONEL OLCOTT
Where is he now?

HPB
He went off to Lancaster to sulk. Seems I'm not giving him enough attention. I've been writing more articles for the newspapers.

COLONEL OLCOTT
It's already starting, I see. Marriage problems.

HPB
It'll be over soon, and I have a hunch I'll have to go back to New York and leave him here. Oh! By the way, now that I got you down to Philadelphia again, come with me to the Holmes séance tonight.

COLONEL OLCOTT
Ah yes, the Holmes. I heard he was a good medium but I read about the controversy in the newspaper. A Dr. Beard really singed them. Says he can imitate everything they do. Are they genuine?

HPB
Genuine Spiritualists, I believe. Dr. Beard is just hot air. All he wants to do is sell his mesmeric healing services. The Holmes are communicating and bringing forth the dead and fallen discarnate forms, hopefully all in the spirit of teaching their sitters that life goes on after the grave. That's all. Everybody seems to want to make more of that simple lesson. Just because these dead folks come back doesn't mean they're divine.

COLONEL OLCOTT
Hah! That's what I concluded from my Eddy experience. They all seem so dumb and far from divine . . . not an ounce of wisdom.

Olcott gets up and walks toward the book cabinet.

COLONEL OLCOTT (CONT'D)
Let's see what that elemental did with the towels.

He smiles mischeviously as he holds up the key and opens the cabinet door. The bundle of towels is lying just where he had placed them weeks ago. He pulls it out and examines a few of the towels.

HPB
Ah! I completely forgot about them.

COLONEL OLCOTT
Well, by God. Look at this. Each and every one of them has been beautifully stitched and hemmed!

He tosses a couple onto HPB's lap.

HPB
Good job. Better than I could do.

COLONEL OLCOTT
You've got little invisible helpers at your command, Mulligan.

HPB
Ah, there is so much to learn about the inner world.

COLONEL OLCOTT
The teachers have come to me at night to show me a whole inner world we can bring into our lives here on earth. God is not outside but resides within all of us, and I can do so much more in life if I tap into that divine power.

HPB
What would your Christian wife say about that? Jesus said the same thing.

COLONEL OLCOTT
I cannot talk to her about all this. I've had to move into my own bedroom, so I can receive these lessons.

HPB
Oh, to change the subject, there is a telegram for you. It arrived this morning.

HPB reaches for the letter from her sewing basket and hands it to him. Olcott with a quizzical look on his face, opens the envelope.

COLONEL OLCOTT
Well, it's going through. Helena, I've got something to confess. It's been bothering me since we met. My marriage is not what I said it was. In fact, I've been living at the Lotus Club in NY for about a year, separate from my family. Mary got wind of an indiscretion I had a year ago. She's filed for divorce. Adultery.

HPB
And your two sons?

COLONEL OLCOTT
That's what this telegram from my office is about. The terms of the divorce. She wants a yearly stipend of $2000 and support for the boys until they finish school. They want to know if I agree, and if so, the proceedings will be fairly quick and easy.

HPB
(smiling slightly)
Now you'll be free from your mortal burdens.

COLONEL OLCOTT
It's my sons I worry about. I want them to be safe and secure. My work and this situation with Mary have taken me away from them. I haven't seen them for a year.

                    HPB
          The Masters will guide you to work out this problem.
          No need to fret, chum. The decision will come
          naturally. It's getting dark and the Holmes seance
          should be starting in an hour. How about more tea
          before we leave?

                                        CUT TO:

INT. HOLMES' SEANCE ROOM IN PHILA. TOWNHOUSE -- THAT SAME NIGHT

Tail end of the séance. A discarnate man, dressed in full regalia of the Russian Csar's elite guard stands in the candlelight in front of the medium's curtained cabinet. His image fades in and out. There's a loud gasp from within the medium's cabinet and a loud thud. The audience stands up, alarmed. THE MEDIUM'S WIFE runs to the cabinet and flings open the curtain, only to find THE MEDIUM HOLMES doubled over and on the floor gasping for breath.

                    LADY FROM AUDIENCE
          Run for a doctor!

                    THE MEDIUM'S WIFE
          No, no. That won't be necessary. He just fell off the
          chair while in trance. Everything's fine. We must end
          the séance. Thank you all for coming. And please do
          not forget to leave your donations in the basket at the
          door!

                                        FADE OUT:

EXT. SIDEWALK PHILA -- LATER

Olcott and HPB walking together on the street after the séance.

                    COLONEL OLCOTT
          Something very curious occurred to me tonight.

                    HPB
          What is that?

                    COLONEL OLCOTT
          These Russian spooks always seem to show up when you're
          in the séance. In the Eddy's séances most of the
          apparitions were run-of-the-mill dead farmers and
          relatives of the audience... that is, until you
          attended.

                    HPB
          What are you implying, my friend?

COLONEL OLCOTT
Did you have something to do with the characters in tonight's séance?

HPB
(smiling wryly)
So those apparitions so shocked the medium himself that he fell off the chair.

COLONEL OLCOTT
(laughing)
But why? You're not a spiritualist.

HPB
I thought I'd spice up the evening a bit. The Masters Kuthumi and Hilarian created the spiritualist experiment to break the grip that death had on western thinking. What better way than to let people talk to the dead!

COLONEL OLCOTT
But most people scoff at these seances.

HPB
Those are mostly the scientific minded, but spiritualism has accomplished its objective: to show survival after death. But some spiritualists are trying to make gods out of these spooks. And as you can see, it's now also a money-making enterprise. Now we must move on to something more substantive. That's our mission, chum. We will introduce a new way of looking at things and in doing so, we may find ourselves one day tearing down many of the Spiritualists assumptions.

COLONEL OLCOTT
And what if the spiritualists don't accept this?

HPB
Of course they won't. I will end up their enemy. I can already see the day when they will denounce me. But in the meantime, I will defend them.

COLONEL OLCOTT
What? Your future enemies?

HPB
Yes, I even wrote an article defending the Holmes' seances against Dr. Beardsley's attacks. Will you get your editor at the Daily Graphics to print it?

COLONEL OLCOTT
You'll never cease to mystify me, Helena. I'll try.

SOUND: We hear the reverberations of the Tibetan prayer bowl leading us to the change of scene.

CUT TO:

EXT. 36 IRVING STREET NEW YORK -- DAY

HPB is waiting on the steps of the building and Olcott hurriedly approaches.

HPB
Is it done?

COLONEL OLCOTT
Yours or mine?

HPB
Both.

COLONEL OLCOTT
Yes, I filed the divorce papers for you, and Betanelly will not contest them, so everything seems in order. In a few weeks, maybe months, it'll be final as you predicted.

HPB
How about yours?

COLONEL OLCOTT
I agreed to Mary's demands. I still must wait until the final decision is rendered. I will have to support Mary and the boys until they are adults.

HPB
Congratulations! Can I ask you something?

COLONEL OLCOTT
Why, yes.

HPB
Did you engineer your indiscretion for the divorce or are you really such a Don Juan?

COLONEL OLCOTT
(looking sheepish)
Yes, it was the only way I could free myself from her. It has not been easy.

HPB
Well, now that we're both going to be free, let us take a look at this apartment. It's not expensive and has a large dining room for us to work in. There's a bedroom downstairs for you and another upstairs for me, so we won't get in each other's way. There's even a maid's room if we can ever afford one.

COLONEL OLCOTT
It sounds perfect. Let's take a look.

CUT TO:

EXT. "THE LAMASERY" (36 IRVING STREET APARTMENT DINING ROOM) -- EVENING

Olcott and HPB nicknamed the Irving Street apartment "The Lamasery" because of the underlying Tibetan Buddhist connection.

INT. "THE LAMASERY" (36 IRVING STREET APARTMENT DINING ROOM) -- EVENING

A few months later . . .

In The Lamasery, 19th Century Victorian dining room with a large rectangular wood dining table with chairs around it. Curtains are red velvet. On the wall where the door leads into the kitchen, there is an old European tapestry. HPB is seated on one end of the table and Olcott on the opposite side. Olcott is rifling through a stack of papers.

HPB
Thank God, that endless stream of visitors stops tonight. Don't answer the doorbell, and we'll have the whole evening to work on the book. . . . that is, unless the Masters send us someone who can add to the text.

COLONEL OLCOTT
I spent the day at the New York Library and checked all the references that your discarnate sources gave us last night. Amazingly they all check out. Even the page numbers. Only slight differences in some page numbers versus the editions that were in the library.

                    HPB
          Good. But wait. I feel them coming through again.
          Yes, it's the professor again sent by Morya.

HPB looks blankly into space and we see a vision of a bespectacled
EUROPEAN GENTLEMAN with a white beard holding a book before HPB.
He opens it and points to some texts. She reads off the pages and
copies the text. The discarnate gentleman turns the page to
indicate other texts he has marked for her.

Meanwhile, Olcott, by this time accustomed to these nightly visits
of discarnate philosophers and savants, nonchalantly edits the
words on the pages HPB flings to him.

A couple hours later . . .

Olcott stands up and stretches. His part of the table is strewn
with bits of paper as he cuts and pastes the master draft.

                    OLCOTT
          You done yet?

HPB holds up her hand.

                    HPB
          One more passage. This should complete the chapter.

She continues to read and copy references from her source in the
space above her place at the table and throws down her pencil when
she's finished.

                    HPB (CONT'D)
          There!

                    COLONEL OLCOTT
          That was good work tonight. What time is it?

                    HPB
          It's already past midnight.

                    COLONEL OLCOTT
          Too bad all the stores are closed. Never mind, it's
          too late and cold out there anyway. But wouldn't it be
          nice to have some fresh grapes to munch on right now?

HPB closes her eyes for a couple minutes. We see her launch a
thought-form into space via visualized word: "Deep purple Hamburgh
grapes". We then see a ball of scintillating atomic particles
engulf the thought-form, breaking the words into the cluster of

particles, then shoot down to a bookshelf in the room. Then a broad wry smile spreads across HPB's face.

                      HPB
         Look behind you, Moloney.

Olcott turns and looks at the bookshelf behind him. We see two large bunches of ripe black Hamburgh grapes hang from the bookshelf.

                COLONEL OLCOTT
         I should have known. What a great chum you are, Mulligan!

He plucks one and savours it, then hands a bunch to HPB. They both enjoy the moment.

                      HPB
         A small respite from the Masters. They are delicious.

                COLONEL OLCOTT
         I still cannot believe all these things are happening before my eyes.

                      HPB
Henry, you still sit there gaping every time this happens. All I did was to launch the idea of those luscious grapes, then the plant elementals whipped up a bunch, that's all. But just remember, all I'm showing you is what every human being will be capable of doing in the New Age. Even you, in whomever you incarnate as. You'll see.

                COLONEL OLCOTT
How come I can't do it now?

                      HPB
You've got more to learn. Besides, this is not your job this time. I bear this burden. These phenomena are a direct result of the spiritual training I received in Tibet. And they take a lot of energy out of you.

                COLONEL OLCOTT
Speaking of rest, chum. Even you need some rest to keep in good health.

                                FADE OUT:

INT. "THE LAMASERY" -- EVENING

Several evenings later . . .SIGNOR B, a thin, wiry Italian in his sixties, dressed in a white suit and Panama hat, enters, one of the daily stream of visitors attracted to the Lamasery.

> SIGNOR B
> Ah! Si. Those days in Italy will remain in our memories forever. Fellow revolutionaries fighting along side Garibaldi. I recognize you, the extraordinary Mme. Blavatsky.

He walks toward HPB with wide open arms.

> HPB
> She's not as extraordinary as you think. What have I done to deserve this visit?

> SIGNOR B
> Only your reputation, Madame, not only on this plane but in the higher dimensions. My Master strongly suggested that I meet you, and upon seeing you in person, I can only say he was right in every way.

Olcott enters the dining room from the kitchen.

> HPB
> This is my colleague Colonel Olcott.

> SIGNOR B
> Ah Hah! You. . You have a colleague? Of course. Pleased to meet you, sir.

Senor B, still standing, shakes Olcott's hands.

> COLONEL OLCOTT
> Please to meet you, sir. What brings you to New York?

> SIGNOR B
> Only to see this extraordinary woman, my friend.

Senor B wanders over to the window balcony off the dining room.

> SIGNOR B (CONT'D)
> What a beautiful clear night. Come, my Colonel friend, come and see this.

Olcott joins him at the window. They both gaze out at the bright moon. Signor B waves his hands to the sky, and then clenches his fists and teeth. His thin body becomes taut and trembles. Seconds later dense black vapours, like thunder clouds seem to cover the moon. Dark rain clouds set in. In a second it begins to rain. No thunder or lightning, no wind, just a downpour outside the window.

> COLONEL OLCOTT
> But . .

Signor B puts his hand on Olcott's arm to quiet him

> HPB
> Well done, Signor B. I couldn't have done better myself. I saw you launch the thought-form and the elementals came at your command.

Signor bows. HPB stands up and sweeps her hand through the air. A white dove flies into the room.

> HPB (CONT'D)
> Look at him closely, Signor. He's not even wet from your rain. And he's alive, in the flesh.

> SIGNOR B
> Bravo! Signorina. I couldn't do better myself. A storm is one thing, but a living animal! Ah! What would our zoologist friends say about that?

> HPB
> They'd probably scoff and call it rabbit-in-the-hat magic trick.

> SIGNOR B
> Then they have no real understanding of the science they study. That being said, I feel I must take my leave now.

> HPB
> Such a short visit. I was just beginning to have to fun.

> SIGNOR B
> (Ignoring HPB's words)
> Colonel Olcott, may I ask you to accompany me downstairs to the corner of the street and point me in the right direction?

> COLONEL OLCOTT
> Certainly.

They both walk out the door.

CUT TO:

EXT. SIDEWALK OUTSIDE THE "LAMASERY" -- NIGHT

                    SIGNOR B
          (hand on Olcott's shoulder and speaking in a low voice)

          I have something important to tell you, a message from
          Master Morya, your Master. Mme. Blavatsky is a very
          dangerous and wicked woman. If you continue to
          associate with her, a great calamity will befall you.

                    COLONEL OLCOTT
          (stepping back with a start)

          Well, Signor, I know the Master Morya; and after seeing
          your phenomena, you might also have some link to the
          Brotherhood; I demand that you give me any sign by
          which I shall know, positively and without room for the
          least doubt, that Mme. Blavatsky is the devil you
          depict, and that the Master's will is that I cease my
          acquaintance with her.

                    SIGNOR B
          Then you do not believe me.

                    COLONEL OLCOTT
          Frankly, no, unless you can produce any sign that can
          convince me.

Signor B's whole body begins to tremble with rage. He stammers and stalks off in a huff.

                                             FADE OUT:

INT. "THE LAMASERY" -- MINUTES LATER

HPB is still working furiously at the dining room table. She hears the bang of the door.

                    HPB
          Back so soon?

                    COLONEL OLCOTT
          Very curious man, indeed. He wanted to tell me that
          you are a very evil and dangerous woman, Mulligan, and
          that a great calamity will befall me if I continue to
          associate with you.

                    HPB
          And what did you tell him?

                    COLONEL OLCOTT
          That nothing could throw black doubt into my heart
          about my friend and guide.

                    HPB
          Bravo, chum. You passed the test! Now you have seen
          for yourself how occult principles can be used by the
          darker side. He can also produce phenomena. He is a
          black magician. That's why I called the white dove in.
          He was floored and had to leave. Now, I'll have to
          write a little love note to Signor B to forget the way
          to my door!

She smiles as looks up into the air for more references and continues writing.

EXT. "THE LAMASERY" -- EVENING

We see the last couple of people filter in the front door as the voice over of Colonel Olcott is heard.

                    COLONEL OLCOTT (V.O.)
          We've called this important meeting of our friends and
          associates to . . .

                                             CUT TO:

INT. THE "LAMASERY" -- EVENING NOVEMBER 17, 1875

The dining room is full of men and women in 19th Century NY dress seated around the large dining table. Olcott is at the head of the table and HPB sits next to him.

                    COLONEL OLCOTT
          . . . to formally constitute a society based on
          Theosophy which comes from the Greek "Theos" or God and
          "sophos" meaning "wise" or the wisdom concerning God.

                    MEMBER 1 IN AUDIENCE
          What do you propose this vehicle to be?

                    COLONEL OLCOTT
          It would be a society of occultists to collect and
          diffuse knowledge about the divine from all sources
          from ancient philosophical and theosophical sources; to
          carry out occult research to show the common source of
          divine inspiration.

> **MEMBER TWO IN AUDIENCE**
> Such a noble venture! I so move that we constitute the Theosophical Society. May God be with us.

> **MEMBER THREE IN AUDIENCE**
> I second.

> **COLONEL OLCOTT**
> Shall we have a show of hands for the vote. . . The vote is unanimous. Thus, is constituted the Theosophical Society. My office will draw up the Preamble and by-laws and duly register this society with the authorities.

> CUT TO:

INT. THE "LAMASERY" -- EVENING

Several months later . .

HPB writing furiously at one end of the dining room. Her scribbling is so fast that the scratching pen seems to fly across pages. We see a masculine arm and hand superimposed on her hand and arm writing. This accounts for the energy and fury by which she writes.

She stops and begins to cut pages into strips of text. Her bottle of paste next to her, she pastes strips of text in another order on a sheet of paper, waves it in the air to dry it, then tosses it over to the other side of the table where Olcott is sitting. Olcott mechanically picks up the paper and tosses it onto a stack of similar cut-and-pasted sheets. It's a production line of book pages.

> **COLONEL OLCOTT**
> I cannot pass this quotation in Chapter 7. I'm sure it cannot read as you have it.

> **HPB**
> Oh, don't bother; it's right; let it pass.

> **COLONEL OLCOTT**
> No, if we're to be credible, we'd better get it exactly right. The pundits will be looking for anything to pick on. You're challenging the very core of their beliefs in materialism.

> **HPB**
> Well, alright. Keep still a minute and I'll try to get the reference for you.

A far-away look comes to HPB's eyes. She shoots a thought-form into the air and we see the words "M. Duncker, *Geschichte des Alterthums* and A. Wuttke, *Geschichte des Heidenthum*." A scintillating ball of atomic light particles engulfs the words and shoots them to the bookshelf.

> HPB (CONT'D)
> There! There, over there; go look for it over there on the bookshelf!"

She points absent-mindedly to the bookshelf where two volumes are lit up while she continues writing. Olcott stands up and fetches them.

> COLONEL OLCOTT
> I was right, Mulligan. The quotes from these books are slightly different. I'll make the changes.

Olcott closes the books, stands up and takes the paper to HPB to show her. We see the two books dissolve into nothing on the table.

HPB nods at the page then resumes her furious writing. Again, we see a masculine hand and arm superimposed upon HPB's hand and arm.

Olcott takes his place again with the stack of cut-and-pasted sheets of text.

The doorbell rings but the two do not stop what they're doing. We hear shuffling of feet while MAGGIE the domestic answers the door and voices in the distance. HPB looks up from her work and smiles. RABBI HOROWITZ, a frequent visitor to the "lamasery" enters.

> HPB
> Rabbi Horowitz! Back again for more! Come sit down next to me. I just received much information about the Kabbala and I want to check some details with you.

> RABBI
> I am at your disposal.

The Rabbi ambles over to HPB and pulls up a chair and the two chat lively.

> HPB
> Rabbi, my collaborator says the occult mysteries contained within the Kabbala cannot be seen by the uninitiated.

> RABBI
> That is right. Only the initiated can see behind the texts. You see, there are secret signs and symbols in the margin that lead the initiated to the deep meanings within.

> HPB
> Does this mean that the commentaries made by the great Josephus, an uninitiated, may be dead letter?

> RABBI
> I'm afraid that may have to be a correct conclusion. My, my, Madame Blavatsky, you will create much controversy if you print that.

> HPB
> I am not here to coddle the reader, but to state the truth.

Again the doorbell rings, and Maggie answers. Olcott turns around mechanically to see who it is. A MR. RAWSON, a renowned expert on Asia Minor arrives.

> COLONEL OLCOTT
> MR. RAWSON! Just the fellow I wanted to talk to.

Olcott gets up and shakes hands.

> COLONEL OLCOTT (CONT'D)
> It's about Lebanese/Syrian Druzes and their leader, Hamsa, whom they call the Messiah. Do you have a few minutes to go over this text with me?

> MR. RAWSON
> Certainly. I see that the book's coming along. My, I've never seen two people work so hard. How long has it been?

> COLONEL OLCOTT
> Just about a year and a half. Working on this book is our nightly dessert. Look here, Mr. Rawson. Mme. Blavaksky states that the leader of the Druzes, Hamsa, was also an embodiment of the Christos and that the soul of Jesus was that of Hamsa.

> MR. RAWSON

>   Those are strong words, my friend, and apt to stir up a
>   lot of anger in the Christians. I never talk about
>   this, but
>
>   (whispering in fear of the unknown, hands trembling
>   slightly)
>
>   I'm afraid Madame is correct. We, in the west, can
>   never admit to this unless we admit to reincarnation.
>   Please excuse me. I believe I've forgotten something.
>   I must be leaving.

Mr. Rawson slinks out the door as if being followed.

>   HPB
>   (shouting across the table)
>   We'll never see him again.

The doorbell rings again, and the domestic answers. We see the Rabbi standing up and putting on his coat.

>   RABBI
>   Madame, whenever you need me, just send me a message.

The Rabbi leaves and a MR. O'SULLIVAN, a researcher of Spiritualist séances, enters.

>   HPB
>   Mr. O'Sullivan! How good to see you. Maggie, bring
>   Mr. O'Sullivan some tea. Come closer. I've added some
>   more text to complete your description of that magical
>   séance in Paris. Here take a look.

Again, the doorbell rings, and yet another guest arrives carrying some books The dining room fills with people going in and out throughout the evening to show how HPB's first book ISIS UNVEILED was written.

>   CUT TO:

INT. "THE LAMASERY"-- COLONEL OLCOTT'S BEDROOM--LATER THAT NIGHT

Olcott is sitting on a chair reading the last pages HPB had handed him before she retired upstairs. Suddenly a bright light takes over the room. He reacts with surprise and out of the bright light, the tall masculine figure of the Master Morya emerges.

Olcott drops to his knees, head bowed. He lifts his head toward the Master with tears in his eyes.

> MORYA
> Arise, O loyal servant of the Brotherhood. It is I who am grateful for your work and service. When we do visit, it is not for the purpose of words but of pure darshan. Words alone can convey precious little. You have met all your obligations and studied diligently under Upasika, for you see, you two are bonded together with me throughout time. More I cannot explain. You are now ready to be transferred from the care of the Brotherhood of Luxor to our Brotherhood of the Himalayas. Our Brothers await your arrival in India.

> COLONEL OLCOTT
> I can make that committment now. If my service is to be India, so be it.

> MORYA
> Your soul is deeply Tibetan from the mountain peaks of the Himalayas, just as Upasika's. So now the pact of love is complete. I honour that pact of the Three. Let it endure through the ages. Just know, I am with you always, even as I am in Darjeeling simultaneously. I leave you a part of myself, never again to be retrieved. I am with you always.

The Master lifts his turban from his head and places it on the small table next to Olcott's chair and disappears.

Sound: Ringing of the Tibetan prayer bowl

EXT. "THE LAMASERY" -- MORNING

A bald, rotundish man, J.W. BOUTON, publisher of the Isis Unveiled knocks loudly on the front door. Maggie, the housekeeper, opens the door and Bouton rushes pass her as she stands shaking her head.

CUT TO:

INT. THE "LAMASERY" -- MORNING SEPTEMBER, 1877

Enter J.W. BOUTON. HPB and Olcott are having breakfast.

                    J.W. BOUTON
          I can't believe it! We have almost sold out of the
          first edition in ten days. Never beyond my wildest
          dreams would I have guessed such a market existed for
          this kind of book! I thought I was going to lose
          money, what with all the changes you and Henry kept
          feeding me. And that's only New York. The whole world
          cries for this book. ISIS UNVEILED is a grand success!

                    COLONEL OLCOTT
          Well, Mulligan, The *New York Herald* called it " one of
          the remarkable productions of the century" and the New
          York Independent stated "The appearance of erudition is
          stupendous."

                    J.W. BOUTON
          That is why the book is selling like hotcakes.

                    HPB
          Great enthusiasm greets a new idea, just like the babe
          in the manger. But as the ideas sink into and roil the
          mass consciousness, the old King Herod thought patterns
          will rear their ugly heads and to try to kill the babe.
          Mr. Bouton, you see success in each book you sell. I
          see each book sold as one more step closer to the
          gallows. My crucifixion has begun.

J.W. Bouton and Colonel Olcott exchange questioning looks.

EXT. "THE LAMASERY" -- CONTINUOUS

Collage with 19th Century period calendar flipping months from
September 1877 to November 1878. Background of calendar shows
people lining up in a NY bookstore to buy Isis Unveiled. Customers
are dressed according to the seasons.

INT. THE "LAMASERY" -- MORNING

(COLONEL OLCOTT, HPB)

Olcott rushes in the door.

                    COLONEL OLCOTT
          Why so glum, Mulligan?

                    HPB
          Birdie is sick.

A listless parakeet lies dying before her on the dining room table.
It breathes its last, shudders and expires.

COLONEL OLCOTT
I'm afraid it's . . .

HPB picks up the bird and holds it against her breasts, rocking and weeping at the same time.

HPB
(crying)
Birdie, birdie. Mama will see you to heaven. You lovely wonder. How much joy you have given me. Go peacefully, my love.

She wraps the bird up in a piece of paper and Olcott sits down and pauses a couple seconds.

COLONEL OLCOTT
Three bits of good news for you, chum, to cheer you up. Your divorce papers from Betanelly came through.

HPB
(smiling)
Thank Heavens!

COLONEL OLCOTT
Second you're now an American citizen! You have to take your oath next week. Can you give up the Russian Emperor for the Constitution!

HPB
Ah! Goodbye, Mother Russia. By the way, Sahib Morya gave me a message from the Master Serapis Bey this morning. We should clear everything by mid-December, December 17 to be exact. What's the third?

COLONEL OLCOTT
Plus this. I got this letter from the Swami Dayanand this morning. They are anxious to be our sister organization in India. They're expecting us and have made an arrangement for a house. So everything is in place. We've just got a couple of months. I need to close down my office and make arrangements for my two sons and Mary.

HPB
You mean Kali. She already suspects you're skipping town. We'd better move fast!

COLONEL OLCOTT
Very funny.

CUT TO:

EXT. "THE LAMASERY" 17 DECEMBER 1878 -- AFTERNOON

A porter from ship SS Canada is exiting with a hand truck full of steamer trunks as Colonel Olcott watches him take them away.

CUT TO:

INT. THE "LAMASERY" 17 DECEMBER 1878 -- AFTERNOON

Olcott returns inside. The apartment is empty and there are two last steamer trunks sitting in the empty dining room.

COLONEL OLCOTT
Last details taken care of. I took the proceeds from the publisher's royalties and bought these steamer tickets. We leave at midnight on the HMS Canada.

Olcott shows the two steamer tickets to HPB

HPB
None too soon to the land of our Mahatmas. Mother India awaits us!

Sound: long ringing of the Tibetan prayer bowl leads to next scene in Bombay India.

CUT TO:

EXT. GATE OF INDIA BOMBAY--ON BOARD THE STEAMER "SPEKE HALL" -- MORNING

January, 1879 Arrival at port of Bombay. Warm mist hangs over the rusty tramp steamer that brought Olcott, HPB, and two other British companions MISS BATES, an unattractive spinster AND MR.WIMBRIDGE, thin wiry artist in his thirties.

We see a small dinghy with three Hindus bearing garlands of flowers pull alongside the steamer. The three Hindues climb up the ladder. Olcott and HPB (who now weighs 250 lbs) are standing on the ship's deck.

                    MOOLJEE THACKERSEY
          Colonel Olcott!

                    COLONEL OLCOTT
          Mr. Mooljee! I almost didn't recognize you. The last
          time I saw you in London you were dressed in a western
          suit. Your Indian attire suits you better. How are
          you, my friend! This is my colleague, Mme Helena
          Blavatsky.

                    MOOLJEE THACKERSEY
          Pleased as ever to see you again after so many letters,
          Colonel. And I am honoured at last to meet the famous
          Mme. Blavatsky! Let me introduce you to PANDIT SHYAMJI
          KRISHNAVARMA AND MR. BALLAJEE SITARAM. They are the
          first members of the Theosophical Society of Bombay!

All three men drape flower garlands over Olcott and HPB

                    COLONEL OLCOTT
          What a pleasure to meet you all! Did Swami Dayanand
          Sarawati come with you? And Mr. Hurrychund?

                    MOOLJEE THACKERSEY
               (looking a bit embarrassed)
          Swamiji could not come but he sends his greetings.
          Hurrychund is busy finalizing the arrangements for you.
          He is preparing the little cottage you requested and
          the carriage to take you there. He will meet us on
          shore. Come let us go.

He claps his hands and coolies run up the gangway to load all the
luggage to take them ashore.

EXT. GATE OF INDIA BOMBAY--ON SHORE -- NOON

Waiting under the burning sun, HURRYCHAND CHITAMON, a tall, rotund
Hindu in his early forties, rushes up to the group. He is one of
the representatives of the Swami Dayanand Sarawati group that
promised to serve as counterparts to the Theosophical Society.

                    HURRYCHUND
          Blessed colleagues. Forgive me for keeping you
          waiting. I am Hurrychund Chitamon.

                    COLONEL OLCOTT
          Finally we meet! After two years of correspondence!
          My esteemed colleague, Mme. Blavatsky.

Hurrychund makes a long and deep bow to HPB.

                              HPB
                    Call me HPB. Now, let's get out of this blazing sun!
                    I'm about to faint.

Hurrychund leads them to a horse-drawn carriage. They pile on. We
see a scrawny coolie standing with a flatbed rickshaw loaded with
the group's steamer trunks in the back of the carriage.

The carriage starts off and the coolie trots behind pulling the
rickshaw. The carriage wends its way through the teeming masses on
Bombay's side streets. Multitudes of people running hither and
yond.

We see Olcott and HPB pointing and drinking in the sights and
colors of the crowded streets. Finally, they reach their
destination in a crowded native quarter teeming with people. They
enter a small courtyard.

EXT. FIRST COTTAGE-- COURTYARD -- DAY

Forlorn courtyard with lush tropical trees and plants. In front of
rundown, dilapidated masonry cottage that once was white but is
covered with mould due to tropical humidity and heat.

                         HURRYCHUND
                    Here we are. This is exactly the cottage you desired,
                    isn't it? It fits the description of everything you
                    wanted in your letter.

                              HPB
                       (looking at Olcott trying to smile)
                    It is lovely.

                         COLONEL OLCOTT
                    It will do. I asked for a small cottage and it's
                    certainly small enough. But I guess after that
                    miserable ship, this looks like Paradise.

                              HPB
                    Hush, Moloney. We're his guests.

                         MISS BATES
                    Can we all fit into it?

                         MR. WIMBRIDGE
                    Have we a choice? At least we don't have to spend
                    another night in the stench on that horrible tramp
                    ship.

                    MISS BATES
          Well, as official housekeeper, I can't wait to clean it
          up. It looks like it can use it! Inside and out.

                    HURRYCHUND
          Come. These servants will make sure you are all
          comfortable. They are at your service. They'll bring
          your trunks in.

                    MISS BATES
          Do they speak English?

                    HURRYCHUND
          No. Except for Babula. Babula, come here!

Hurrychund claps his hands and Babula, a Hindu in his teens, rushes
out from the shade of the trees.

                    HURRYCHUND (CONT'D)
          This is Miss Bates, the housekeeper. She will tell you
          what you need to do.

Babula's looks frightened as he nods to Miss Bates.

                    HURRYCHUND (CONT'D)
          Babula is especially gifted with languages. He will
          learn English from you very quickly.

A bewildered Miss Bates and Mr. Wimbridge wander into the little
cottage while Olcott and HPB look around the courtyard like two
excited children

                    COLONEL OLCOTT
          Not quite what we expected but nonetheless our home in
          India.

                                                            FADE OUT:

EXT. FIRST COTTAGE IN BOMBAY -- MORNING

A week later. . .

We see throngs gathered in the streets outside the humble compound.
Drums are beating. People press against the compound gate trying
to get a glimpse of the people inside.

EXT. FIRST COTTAGE IN BOMBAY --INSIDE THE COURTYARD -- MORNING

Some 300 chairs are arranged in front of the cottage veranda. All seats are filled. HPB is sitting on the veranda and Olcott is standing and just finishing his speech.

> COLONEL OLCOTT
> . . . and so my friends, this will serve as the temporary home and headquarters of the Theosophical Society in Bombay. We remain open to all religions and all faiths, for we all share the same Source of inspiration--the Trans-Himalayan Brotherhood. So let us begin a new era marked by the east melding with the west.

Applause loud and enthusiastic.

> MAN IN AUDIENCE
> (standing)
> We came to see some magic.

> ANOTHER MAN
> Yes, show us something. Show us some miracles of the Brotherhood!

> WOMAN IN THE AUDIENCE
> Show us if your Brotherhood is real.

> AUDIENCE
> Show us! Show us!

We see HPB sitting on the veranda. She shakes her head and feigns a smile. The audience eggs her on. Finally, she stands up and looks into space. Silence overtakes the audience.

She stares into space. We see the thought-form in words "Tibetan temple bells". With her right hand she motions to a scintillating ball of light particles which swoop over the thought-form and transform it into Tibetan bells. The little bells start ringing right over the heads of a few people in the audience. People try to reach for and swat the space above their heads to capture the bells. She sweeps her hand toward the the grumpiest and stodgiest in the audience and signals the bells to tinkle above their heads. The audience is delighted.

> AUDIENCE (CONT'D)
> More! More!

Olcott looks at HPB and she nods her head.

> HPB
> (muttering to herself and Olcott))

> The road will be long indeed to bring them from this fascination for bells into deep occult thinking. God be with us. Let this open the eyes of the few who realize where it comes from.

We watch HPB as she concentrates deeply and we see her project from her mind the thought-form "white doves" into the air. Again, the atomic particles swoop around the thought-form which like clay are formed into white doves.

The audience quiets to a whisper, unaware of what is going on. Then HPB gestures broadly over the expectant audience, and dozens of white doves suddenly swoop down from the sky over them. A momentary chaos erupts as the audience ducks the incoming doves but they are momentarily thrilled.

Hurrychund moves quickly in front of the crowd and claps his hands to gather the audience's attention. Then a colourful procession of dancers and drummers enter the courtyard.

We see HPB regain her seat on the verandah

> **HPB (CONT'D)**
> That was all they wanted, Moloney. A magic show. I wonder if there is at least one of them that questions where those doves came from!
>
> **COLONEL OLCOTT**
> Patience, chum. The Masters never said this mission would be easy. It will take time.

FADE OUT:

INT. FIRST COTTAGE IN BOMBAY -- MORNING

A week later . . .

> **COLONEL OLCOTT**
> Look at this headline! They are denouncing you now as a Russian spy. It's here on the front page.
>
> **HPB**
> What?
>   (expletives)
>
> **COLONEL OLCOTT**
> It says here that the founders of the Theosophical Society must be considered suspicious, "for they bury themselves in the filthy native quarters". This lays

credence to what some say: that Madame Blavatsky is a Russian spy!

                    HPB
          Oh, is that right?
                    (expletives)
          Bastards. Ever since that crowd gathered here last
          week, I keep seeing the same man loitering around
          outside the compound. Look over there, Moloney. Wait.
          You'll see him pass the entrance from time to time. My
          intuition tells me we're under observation by the
          British authorities. There!

She points to a well-dressed Hindu lurking outside the compound gate.

                    COLONEL OLCOTT
          All I see is Hurrychund at the gate. He's waving.
          Wave to him.

Hurrychund, smiling broadly, carries a briefcase and walks briskly up to the two sitting on the veranda.

                    HURRYCHUND
          Is there something I can get you two? Some coffee?

                    COLONEL OLCOTT
          Yes, why not?

                    HURRYCHUND
                    (he claps his hands)
          Babula! Bring more coffee for the sahibs and a cup for
          me!

Hurrychund draws another chair from the veranda and sits next to Olcott and HPB.

                    HURRYCHUND (CONT'D)
          Heh! Heh! Beautiful morning, isn't it? Heh, heh. I
          have a few small matters to cover with you.

                    COLONEL OLCOTT
          Yes, we also wanted to discuss our cooperation with the
          Arya Samaj and the Swami Dayanand.

                    HURRYCHUND
          Ah, yes. But first . . .

COLONEL OLCOTT
We sent you some money to show our good faith in cooperating with your group. But we've not heard a word from the Swami. Nor have we had the pleasure of meeting him.

HURRYCHUND
Ah, yes. We wish to make the Arya Samaj organization your home in India. The Swami will take this matter up with you later. But I have some other business to review with you first.

He fishes in his briefcase.

HURRYCHUND (CONT'D)
This is the bill for everything up to now.

HPB
What bill? Let me see that.

She snatches the bill from Hurrychund's hand.

HPB (CONT'D)
Look at this, Henry.

COLONEL OLCOTT
600 Rupees! For what?

HURRYCHUND
Sahib, For the carriage from the port, the rickshaw, the porters, the rent for the cottage, the dancers and drummers for the celebration, the rental of the 300 chairs for the guests, the food we served them, . . . all inclusive. I gave you the best prices.

HPB
But, but, Mr. Hurrychund. I thought we were your guests. Guests of the Swami.

HURRYCHUND
Ah, yes. But someone has to pay for all that has occurred.

COLONEL OLCOTT
But all we asked for was this cottage and for Babula's salary, not all the public celebrations.

HURRYCHUND
Yes, but this is part of our way of welcoming foreigners. We wanted you to feel welcomed. All this is included in this bill.

HPB
We must pay for our own welcome? We would never do this in Russia . . . or in America.

HURRYCHUND
But someone has to pay for all this. We are poor. You have money.

COLONEL OLCOTT
Then, who owns this house and courtyard?

HURRYCHUND
I do. You can see it is a small and humble cottage. It's all I've got and I gave it to you.

COLONEL OLCOTT
What about the Swami of Arya Samaj?

HURRYCHUND
I am part of their group.

COLONEL OLCOTT
I see. Is that why we haven't met the Swami yet? I mean, you wanted to do your business with us first?

HPB
Exploit us, you mean.

Hurrychund lowers his head and doesn't answer.

COLONEL OLCOTT
What about all the money we sent you from New York for the Arya Samaj and the Swami?

HPB stands up.

HPB
(swearing)
You stole that money, didn't you? And you now want us to pay for this joyous welcome you've given us?

Hurrychund remains silent.

                    COLONEL OLCOTT
          So you wanted to keep us pigeons for yourself, exploit
          us, before we could meet the Swami. No. We will not
          pay you one more cent, until YOU return the money we
          sent you.

                    HPB
               (screaming expletives)
          What the hell?

Babula hears the commotion and comes running out.

                    BABULA
          Madame, Sahib, what is wrong?

                    HPB
          Never mind, Babula. Go outside and call Mooljee.
          We're moving tomorrow. And Mr. Hurrychund, I will see
          to it that the Swami himself of the Arya Samaji knows
          of your criminal actions.

                    HURRYCHUND
               (clasping his hands in a prayer position)
          Are you going to pay me?

                    COLONEL OLCOTT
          We will do a final accounting after you return the
          money we sent you in the name of the Theosophical
          Society to the Arya Samaji.

                                                       CUT TO:

INT. SECOND COTTAGE BOMBAY -- DAY

Second cottage is located down the road from the first one in the
same native quarters. A few days later . . .

HPB and Olcott are sitting on the small veranda of the small modest
house surrounded by palms and lush tropical plants.

                    HPB
          Well, Moloney. I guess we're finally in the Bombay
          quarters of the Theosophical Society. May we prosper
          in this humble place.

She lifts her teacup and toasts Olcott.

                    COLONEL OLCOTT
          The garden is very agreeable, isn't it? We were lucky
          to find this house in such a rush. By the way, we
          received a very nice letter this morning from a Mr.
          Percy Sinnett, editor-in-chief of the Pioneer, one of
          the most influential Anglo-Indian newspapers.

                    HPB
          Well, that's a switch. All the other Anglo Indian
          newspapers have been vicious toward us, accusing me of
          being a Russian spy. Is he connected to one of these
          Christian missions, too?

                    COLONEL OLCOTT
          It doesn't look like it. He extends an invitation to
          the both of us to visit him and his wife in Allahabad.
          He says he's already investigated some mediumistic
          phenomena in London, so it looks like he's sincere in
          wanting to pursue more occult questions.

                    HPB
          Yes, the Masters are urging us to accept this
          invitation. It may be the way we can penetrate British
          "society", as they say here among the snobs of the
          English hierarchy. But first I have something pressing
          to do. Babula, come!

She claps her hands and Babula comes running.

                    HPB (CONT'D)
          Find Mooljee and tell him to get a horse and carriage.
          I must go somewhere.

                    COLONEL OLCOTT
          Where are you going?

                    HPB
          You will know after we get back. I must go
          immediately.

She gets up, leaving Olcott with a bewildered look on his face.

                                                       CUT TO:

INT. INSIDE A HORSE-DRAWN CARRIAGE -- DAY

Focus on HPB. Mooljee is seated opposite her. We follow the
carriage as it winds its way through the crowded streets. HPB
barks out precise directions and Mooljee translates her orders to
the driver.

                    MOOLJEE THACKERSEY
          But, Madame, how do you know where to go? You've never
          been here before.

                    HPB
          Hush! Just tell the driver where I want him to go.

We see the carriage making its way through the crowded streets and
then on a rough dirt road along the seaside. They finally arrive
at a gated white mansion with a stately portico supported by which
Ionic pillars. In front of the portico two gardeners tend a lush
rose garden. The whole property glows with a golden light that is
brighter than the outside.

                    HPB (CONT'D)
          Stop! This is the place.

EXT. THE WHITE MANSION--MAIN GATE -- DAY

We see HPB struggle off the carriage and speak to one of the
gardeners who opens the gate into the garden. As she walks up to
the portico, we see the tall and stately Rajput Indian, El Morya,
emerge from the house all dressed in white. They greet each other
like old friends and retire into the mansion.

                                                  CUT TO:

EXT. THE WHITE MANSION--NEXT TO CARRIAGE -- DAY

We see Mooljee standing next to carriage and talking to the driver.

                    MOOLJEE THACKERSEY
          What is this place?

                    DRIVER
          I don't know. First time I come here.

Mooljee beckons one of the gardeners to come to the gate. The
gardners are reluctant, but Mooljee keeps beckoning. Finally, one
of them approaches the gate.

                    MOOLJEE THACKERSEY
          Who lives in this house?

The gardener shrugs and signals he does not understand. He motions
the other gardener to come to the gate, but he refuses. Mooljee
remains completely bewildered.

MOOLJEE THACKERSEY (CONT'D)
Who is this Sahib?

Still no answer. Mooljee paces back and forth in front of the gate.

WIDE ANGLE: HPB emerges from the front door. She bows reverently to the tall Indian who motions to the gardener. The gardener rushes up with a bunch of roses for HPB. HPB takes the roses and cradles them in her arms. She bows to her host, then walks back to the carriage.

INT. CARRIAGE -- DAY

Carriage turns around and heads back their compound.

CUT TO:

INT. SECOND COTTAGE IN BOMBAY -- EARLY AFTERNOON

MOOLJEE THACKERSEY
The driver said he's never seen that house before.

COLONEL OLCOTT
You visited a house that doesn't exist?

MOOLJEE THACKERSEY
But I am sure I can find it again.

HPB enters the room and joins the conversation.

HPB
We'll wager you 100 rupees. Go with the same driver and look for it.

MOOLJEE THACKERSEY
It's a wager. I remember all your directions.

Mooljee walks briskly out to join the driver outside.

Colonel Olcott glances over to HPB and sees her mischevious smile. She winks.

> COLONEL OLCOTT
> Knowing you, he'll never find it. By the way, we received a letter from the Swami Dayanand while you were gone this morning. I am sure they know about Hurrychund's attempt to cheat us. However, they still want to be our sister organisation in India, but on condition we follow their regulations.

HPB pulls up a chair to examine the letter.

> HPB
> After this experience with Hurrychund, I have doubts. Swamiji hasn't made much of an effort to come to see us. Just sending that scoundrel Hurrychund to cheat us.

> COLONEL OLCOTT
> Look at these rules. What do you think?

> HPB
> (looking through the list of rules)
> This would be unacceptable! As a their sister organization we would not be allowed to mix with Buddhists, Parsis, Zoroastrians or any others, only Hindus.

> COLONEL OLCOTT
> That's not what he wrote in the letters he sent us in New York. Maybe Hurrychand wrote them, so he could snag us to cheat us. But these rules! They reversed what we agreed to before we came here. This tastes the same as that Hurrychund fellow. Well, chum, I don't know about you, but I can't agree to these terms.

> HPB
> No, the Theosophical Society must stand on its own. This is what the Masters have reaffirmed. So that's it, Moloney. We'll have to let the Swami know we can't associate with his organization.

FADE OUT:

INT. SECOND COTTAGE IN BOMBAY -- LATER THAT AFTERNOON

Mooljee runs up to the veranda where Colonel Olcott and HPB are sitting. HPB is furiously fanning herself.

MOOLJEE THACKERSEY
We looked everywhere. It wasn't there. And we followed the same route there. How can a whole house disappear like that?

HPB
You would have seen the mansion again had not a veil been brought to block your sight.

MOOLJEE THACKERSEY
I saw it the first time. I spoke to the gardeners. They were not real?

HPB
Like all spots inhabited by Adepts of the Brotherhood, a circle of illusion is formed around it and guarded by elementals in service. This particular bungalow is kept as an occasional resting and meeting place for Gurus and Chelas of the Brotherhood when traveling.

MOOLJEE THACKERSEY
So I did see it.

HPB
Yes, you had the privilege of seeing it as the veil was lifted when we stopped the carriage there yesterday. It is like all the buried ancient libraries, hoards of treasure to be used in the future for the purposes of the Brotherhood must be kept hidden until Karma requires its restoration to human use.

COLONEL OLCOTT
Shall we call this an unfair wager, old chum?

HPB
Not on your life. I'm not making excuses for Mooljee! He still couldn't find the mansion. Nevertheless,
    (turning to Mooljee)
Keep the 100 rupees and promise me you will it for the good of the people around you.

MOOLJEE THACKERSEY
I'll donate it to the Theosophical Society. That's where the greatest goodwill comes . . . especially after this experience.

                    COLONEL OLCOTT
          Rightly said.

                                              FADE OUT:

EXT. SECOND COTTAGE IN BOMBAY -- AFTERNOON

Heavy monsoon rains pour down. Olcott and HPB are sitting on the veranda enjoying the rain. A tall young gaunt, skinny Hindu man, DAMODAR, approaches the cottage wearing a white rubber raincoat with hood, leggings on pencil thin legs.

                    COLONEL OLCOTT
          Who is this strange man coming our way?

                    HPB
          He looks like a stick man.

                    DAMODAR
          Pardon me. But you must be the famous Mme. Blavatsky
          and Colonel Olcott.

                    HPB
          Yes, yes, come out of the rain, young man. Take off
          your rain gear and sit down here next to me.

Damodar struggles out of his raincoat as it is hot and sticky. He is rail thin.

                    DAMODAR
               (heavy Indian accent)
          My name is Damodar K. Mavalankar. I read your book,
          ISIS Unveiled, and since then it is no exaggeration to
          say that I have been a really living man only these few
          months; for between life as it appears to me now and
          life as I comprehended it before, there is an
          unfathomable abyss. You see, I aspired only for
          acquiring land and riches, social position, like my
          family. I don't want those things anymore.

                    HPB
          Then what can we do for you?

                    DAMODAR
          I want to serve. I want to learn more from you.
          Seeing you two finally here, I never want to leave.

HPB looks at Olcott. They both nod.

                    HPB
          Then join us. Come live with us. We have a small room
          we can give you. Judging from your command of English,
          you must have had good schooling.

                    DAMODAR
          Yes, m'am. I have been to the best schools money can
          buy in India, and for that I am thankful for. I come
          from a Brahmin family. If I stay in your house, I will
          be violating our rules of caste. They will probably
          disown me. But I don't care, for what I feel in my
          heart is more right than these rules.

                    HPB
          You could help us on the publication of the
          Theosophist, our new magazine for the society.

Tears begin to fill Damodar's eyes.

                    DAMODAR
          If you only knew what an honour that would be for me.

                                              FADE OUT:

INT. SECOND COTTAGE IN BOMBAY -- MORNING

Olcott and HPB taking breakfast on the veranda

                    HPB
          Received this letter in the morning mail from an old
          friend, Emma Coulomb, from Egypt. She and her husband
          owned a hotel in Cairo where I stayed and they helped
          me a lot while I was there. They're Colombo.

                    COLONEL OLCOTT
          Ceylon? That's quite a distance from Egypt. What does
          she want?

                    HPB
          She heard we set up the Theosophical Society and wants
          to know if we can sponsor her and Alexis to come work
          with us. They're destitute in Ceylon.

                    COLONEL OLCOTT
          We already have Miss Bates, who, by the way, has not
          stopped grumbling about everything since we got here,
          including Wimbridge. My god, these two fight all the
          time. Even the ducks out back get upset. Add two more
          and we'll have a zoo of scrapping ducks and humans
          here. There's no room for them.

> HPB
> I'd like to help them as they helped me at one time.

> COLONEL OLCOTT
> I would advise no. It sounds like a lot of trouble.

> HPB
> We need to do something to help them.

> COLONEL OLCOTT
> Suit yourself. But I smell trouble. But maybe we can see them in Ceylon next month. I'd like to meet them before we make a decision.

> HPB
> Fair enough, Moloney.

> COLONEL OLCOTT
> But first, remember, we've still got take that trip to Allahabad to visit that journalist, Sinnett. He wrote again saying he and his wife are expecting us with great anticipation.

> HPB
> That's a change. British "Society" now wants an audience with the Theosophical Society.

SOUND: Ringing of Tibetan prayer bowl leads us out of Bombay and into Indian provinces.

CUT TO:

INSERT: Stock takes of 19th Century Indian steam engine and train making its way through the Indian countryside, crowded train cars, crowded train stations.

EXT. ALLAHABAD TRAIN STATION-- AFTERNOON

December, 1879

We see a steam locomotive pulling a train into the Allahabad station. Hordes on the platform rush toward the moving train draggin their belongings in order to grab a place on the roof and window sills of the train even before it stops. Station officials blow their whistles to prevent them and establish order, but to no avail. Passengers, including Olcott, HPB fight their way off the train as new passengers fight to get on. A typical train arrival.

EXT. PLATFORM TRAIN STATION ALLAHABAD -- AFTERNOON MINUTES LATER

Olcott, HPB, Damodar, and Babula stand on the platform of the Allahabad train station, a section roped off for white people. We see a pair of horses and a barouche with driver and two liveried footmen stand in the background. A distinguished looking A.P. SINNETT, a man in his forties but looking older with moustache, steps forward to greet the travelers.

> A.P. SINNETT
> I am delighted you accepted my invitation and on behalf of the *Pioneer* news journal and of course my wife, Patience, I welcome you to Allahabad.

> COLONEL OLCOTT
> I'm Henry Olcott. We are honoured, Mr. Sinnett. May I present my colleague, Madame Helena Blavatsky.

> A.P. SINNETT
> Much honoured. You come with much controversy swirling around you since your arrival in India. We journalists love these kinds of personages. Welcome, madame.

HPB laughs out loud. Everyone climbs into the barouche and as they drive off, they leave the station in a cloud of dust which the masses must swallow.

INT. SINNETT'S BAROUCHE--MINUTES LATER

> HPB
> (whispering)
> Did you see that man?

> COLONEL OLCOTT
> What man?

> HPB
> The one who thinks I'm a spy. He was at the train station. I saw him when we got off the train.

> COLONEL OLCOTT
> He's followed us all the way here? This is outrageous.

FADE OUT:

INT. SINNETT'S HOME IN ALLAHABAD--DINING ROOM -- EVENING

Mr. and MRS PATIENCE SINNETT (a beautiful, charming woman) along with guests, MR A.O. HUME (a stodgy, stiff, government official and later one of the founders of the Indian Congress Party) MRS HUME (presumably an alcoholic), HPB and Olcott are getting up from an elegantly set dinner table and walking toward the parlour.

INT. SINNETT'S HOME IN ALLAHABAD--PARLOUR -- EVENING

>   HPB
>   (Whispering to Olcott))
>   The smell of alcohol is making me ill.
>
>   COLONEL OLCOTT
>   Not so loud. We're their guests.
>
>   HPB
>   Don't worry. But look at the way they all drink! Mrs.
>   Hume is already teetering and slurring her words.
>
>   COLONEL OLCOTT
>   Hush! Enough.
>
>   PATIENCE SINNETT
>   Madame Blavatsky, your fame has followed you here. Can
>   you grace us with an example of your phenomenal
>   manifestations?
>
>   HPB
>   (shakes her head in the negative)
>   Why spoil a perfectly wonderful and relaxing evening?
>
>   HUME
>   That can only be complemented by something of the
>   extraordinary, I might add. My, what was that?
>   Sounded like some bells.

Tibetan bells tinkle just above his head. The stodgy Hume starts swatting the air above his head. Then louder raps click from under his seat. A look of momentary panic streaks across his face. He loses his stiff, stodgy composure and jumps up. His wife titters, then doubles over with laughter as she watches her husband jump around, swatting the bells in mid-air. Then the sound of raps come from under her seat and she jumps up. Everyone joins in laughing as the bells and rapping cause bedlum in the parlour. They're all reduced to curious children swatting the space above them and trying to grab hold of the bells.

                    HUME (CONT'D)
               (red-faced with embarrassment)
          Well, one could say I got what I asked for.

                    PATIENCE SINNETT
          Where are those bells? Oh, my God, they're above my
          head now.

                    A.P. SINNETT
          Now, there's a rapping above my head.

We see HPB wink to Olcott as they both turn toward the kitchen door where the Indian servants have gathered to watch in amazement their white "masters" lose control of themselves. Olcott lets out a hoot as he sees their shocked faces.

                    HPB
               (laughing along with Olcott)
          That's why we're here-- to break down social
          convention. We're all basically children!

                    HUME
          Well, that settles it. Henry, you must give a lecture
          about these things to our community here. I'll arrange
          it.

                                                  CUT TO:

EXT. MAYO HALL ALLAHABAD-- EVENING

A few days later . . .

INSERT: Poster announcing "What is Theosophy?" On wall of Mayo Hall.

INT. MAYO HALL ALLAHBAD-- STAGE -- EVENING

We see Olcott on the stage as he concludes his speech. A crowd rushes onto the stage and surrounds Olcott.

EXT. MAYO HALL ALLAHABAD-- EVENING

A.P. Sinnett, A.O. Hume, Mrs. Hume, Patience Sinnett and HPB are exiting the Hall. They climb into Sinnett's Barouche. HPB is very agitated.

                    HPB
          Moloney, I was shocked at your behaviour in there.

> OLCOTT
> What did I do?

> HPB
> You kissed that Indian woman's hand.

> OLCOTT
> I was just being gallant.

> HPB
> Have you no shame? In front of her husband and family. She was very beautiful, and you lost control, Jack.

> OLCOTT
> We can discuss this later, please.

> HPB
> No, I want to discuss this now.
>   (expletives)

The rest of the party in the carriage sits stunned as HPB rants like a mad woman at Olcott all the way back to the Sinnett's home.

                        FADE OUT:

INT. SINNETT'S HOME IN ALLAHBAD--LIBRARY -- LATER THAT EVENING

AP Sinnett and A.O. Hume are smoking cigars and drinking a nightcap.

> HUME
>   (whispering)
> Have they retired? That was quite a display of temper tonight. I could hear her going on upstairs.

> A.P. SINNETT
> Very disturbing. She warned me that she was a rough old hippo. And of course what the Colonel did to that pretty Hindu woman was unconscionable. It's the kind of familiarity we British would never show a native.

> HUME
> But still, does it merit such a tongue-lashing in front of everyone? Lack of control, I'd say. What if she does the same to any of us in public? Really, I wonder why have these so-called Masters sent such people to India?

A.P. SINNETT

Ostensibly to start an eclectic spiritual society espousing that all major religions are basically the same esoterically and from the same source, thus laying the basis for a world brotherhood of sorts.

HUME
(laughing)

They must have had a shock when they visited their first Hindu temple. I mean, to see that Pantheon of gods piled on one another. Some with those awful, ghastly faces. How can they reconcile all of them to the saints of the Catholic Church?

A.P. SINNETT

Never. But I gather they are quite anti-Christian and more sympathetic toward the Hindus and Buddhists. It's strange because the Colonel is 100% American and she's of Russian origin, although just naturalized American. Quite a pair.

HUME

At times, she has the markings of an aristocrat but my, she does seem to lose complete control of her temper. Fiery temper. A tempest.

A.P. SINNETT

Colonel Olcott certainly bears all those tantrums with wonderful fortitude. Do you think they are a couple?

HUME
(smiling wryly)

Certainly not! Can't you tell? There's not one bit of passion between the two.

A.P. SINNETT

They'll be leaving tomorrow for Bombay. I must say they've created quite a stir here in this quiet town. Patience and I have welcomed the stir from our humdrum life here.

HUME

I have a feeling we'll be seeing more of them in the future. Please give them our regards when you see them off tomorrow.

SOUND: Ringing of Tibetan prayer bowl brings us back to Bombay.

CUT TO:

INT. THIRD HOUSE IN BOMBAY CALLED THE CROW'S NEST -- MORNING

While HPB and Olcott were traveling, the staff found another more accommodating house. This new home is called the Crow's Nest located on a hill in Bombay which affords them more space and a respite from the crowded teeming quarters of their previous house. The home is still simple and basic but more airy as it is located on a knoll and surrounded by tropical plants and trees.

Babula and a European couple appear at the door of the small dining room where HPB and Olcott are taking their breakfast.

> HPB
> Emma! What are doing here in Bombay? We were planning to meet you in Ceylon next month. This is Colonel Olcott.

> COLONEL OLCOTT
> Yes, we were not expecting you. How did you arrive?

> EMMA COULOMB
> The missionaries took up a collection and paid for our passage here. Please help us. We're destitute. Find my husband any kind of work. I can be your housekeeper. He can fix anything. We ran a hotel together and we'll turn this place into something you would be proud of.

ALEXIS COULOMB shakes his head, contrite, hat in hand.

Emma Coulomb throws herself down on her knees and kisses HPB's feet.

> HPB
> No need for that, EMMA. Please get up. So pleased to see you and Alexis again.

> EMMA COULOMB
> I am so grateful to you, Helena. It's been a long, long time since Egypt. Thank you for taking us in.

Olcott glares at HPB.

> HPB
> Can you two please wait outside on the veranda? I have something to discuss with my colleague.

The Coulombs shuffle out to the veranda.

COLONEL OLCOTT
Did you do this?

HPB
Of course not. They just appeared. I couldn't refuse them. The Mahatmas said they could be of help to us. And they're destitute!

COLONEL OLCOTT
What do you want me to do?

HPB
You figure it out as you always do so well, chum.

COLONEL OLCOTT
If she takes over the household, what should we do with Miss Bates? She's bad enough with her foul personality spoiling the whole ambiance of this household.

HPB
Let's make Bates the sub-editor of the Theosophist? She can help Damodor and me with my writing, like our secretary.

COLONEL OLCOTT
I wasn't aware she had any literary or secretarial talents.

HPB
But we have no choice. They're begging us to help them.

COLONEL OLCOTT
Why does this have to happen to us just when we're about to leave for Ceylon? We'll take Wimbridge with us. That will be one less here to cause battle. I have a bad feeling about this whole arrangement.

HPB
Moloney, you worry too much. What will be, will be. Look at it as two angels who may have been sent to us to help us.

COLONEL OLCOTT
You mean two dark angels! I hope this place is still standing when we get back from Ceylon.

CUT TO:

INT. COULOMB QUARTERS IN THE CROW'S NEST--LATER THAT DAY

> EMMA COULOMB
> I could tell that Olcott doesn't want us around. You'd better be extra nice to him, Alexis. Make sure you do everything he wants.

> ALEXIS COULOMB
> Don't worry. I'll make him happy we're here.

> EMMA COULOMB
> But first we have to get rid of the Bates lady and Wimbridge. They're already two too many here.

> ALEXIS COULOMB
> But they're friends of Helena's.

> EMMA COULOMB
> Don't worry. I'll take care of them. I sense Helena has a good thing going here. It's an opportunity for us, too.

> ALEXIS COULOMB
> How is that?

> EMMA COULOMB
> She can do these magic tricks and thrill people, especially the bored, rich ones. They'll invite them into their parlours. It's a good way to enter the the world of the rich and powerful. I think we've struck gold.

SOUND: Ringing of Tibetan prayer bowl leads us to Ceylon.

FADE OUT:

EXT. STEAM SHIP DOCKS AT COLOMBO PORT -- MORNING

Tumultuous arrival of HPB and Olcott organized by Buddhist leaders at the port. Hundreds of shaven Buddhist monks in saffron robes are lined up on the dock to meet the visitors. There is a line of monks with drums beating a greeting rhythm while the monks chant. There are also some western men in white tropical suits and their wives in long 18th Century western dresses with parasols to ward off the intense tropical sun. The white people, most likely Christian missionaries, are roped off from the dark people and the monks in their special zone and await their own contingent of missionaries. By their body language, i.e. backs to the monks, we can see the disdain the missionaries have for the Buddhist "pagans".

CUT TO:

EXT. OPEN PAVILION ON A COCONUT PLANTATION-- DAY

A large rectangular building located in the middle of a coconut plantation and built of teak columns and a thatched roof of coco branches is besieged with hordes of native Singhalese. We see HPB sitting with many older saffron-clad monks on the platform behind Olcott as he finishes a brief address. Seated stiffly in the front row are English and American Christian missionaries.

> COLONEL OLCOTT
> And so, my friends, the Theosophical Society supports your efforts to revive your ancient heritage of Theravada Buddhism in the school system here in Ceylon. This long tradition cannot be allowed to die in the minds of your children.

Applause from the audience. One of the Christian missionaries stands up and turns to the audience.

> MISSIONARY
> Frauds! These are devil worshipers. Do not listen to them. I am ashamed to admit that he is a fellow countryman. Shame on him.

> MISSIONARY 2
> This is Satan incarnate. Our schools are your salvation, not theirs.

> HEAD MONK
> (Standing up)
> Yes, yes, my friends. Please have a seat. All westerners are our friends even if we do not agree with all of them. We endorse the ideas of Colonel Olcott and Mme. Blavatsky who deeply respect our religion.

There is a loud applause. The front row of missionaries stand up and march out of the assembly. The Head Monk waits for them to leave, then raises both hands.

> HEAD MONK (CONT'D)
> Now, for those who have come for a healing, Colonel Olcott will spend the rest of the afternoon healing those who are most in need. Please line up on the right side.

The crowd presses against the stage while younger monks organize the people to line up.

INT. OPEN PAVILION ON A COCONUT PLANTATION-- DAY

A long line of sick and infirm snakes through the coconut grove. We see Olcott seated in the pavilion. He uses his hands to pass over individuals who are blind, deaf, crippled etc. Most receive healings and relief and there are cries of joy when a cripple throws down his cane and walks away.

INT. OPEN PAVILION ON A COCONUT PLANTATION-- EVENING

> HEAD MONK
> (approaching Olcott)
> It is time to stop. You must be exhausted.

> COLONEL OLCOTT
> There is still a long line. I can take them after a good night's sleep.

> HEAD MONK
> Come. I will tell the people to come back tomorrow afternoon. In the morning, we have our ceremony for you. Come and rest and take some food.

>> FADE OUT:

EXT. CEYLON A HUGE BUDDHIST TEMPLE-- NEXT DAY

We enter through a great arch of greenery bearing the words "Welcome to the founders of the Theosophical Society" erected over the main entrance of the temple compound.

INT. A HUGE BUDDHIST TEMPLE-- DAY

We see Olcott and HPB kneeling before a huge golden statue of the Buddha in order to "take Pansil", or the oath of Buddhism. An old monk reads out a series of sentences in the Pali language, and Olcott and HPB repeat them with difficulty.

EXT. A HUGE BUDDHIST TEMPLE -- DAY

HPB and Olcott emerge from the temple to the cheers of a crowd of about 100 schoolgirls and boys from the temple's school and monks. They line the path leading to the temple and throw flowers to HPB and Olcott as they come out. The children, at the prompting of their teachers, begin singing a Singhalese song.

> HPB
> I wonder if they think we're being married.

                    COLONEL OLCOTT
Sometimes you say the silliest things, HPB. They know
what "Taking Pansil" is all about.

                    HPB
Henry, we must be serious about what we're doing. We
muefst remember that our Buddhism is that of the
Master-Adept Gautama and a philosophy, not a creed
which is what most of this form of Buddhism is. We
must be clear in our minds that we do not endorse this
southern form of Buddhism over the Tibetan form from
which we come.

                    COLONEL OLCOTT
Let that distinction remain in our minds as our hosts
would probably not agree with us! Now, let's join the
celebration.

                    HPB
Our taking pansil will enrage the Christian
missionaries even more. So we burn in hell together!
I say let them eat crow. Did you see the missionaries
watching you heal the other day? Even after they had
stalked out of the assembly.

                    COLONEL OLCOTT
No, I was too busy.

                    HPB
They were red with jealousy. You, my friend, the so-
called heathen, were healing like their Jesus. What a
comedy! They preacheth the bible, yet healeth not!

                    COLONEL OLCOTT
Even if they've disrupted so many of our meetings and
used the newspapers to slander us, the push to
reinstate Buddhism in the schools will come from our
Buddhist friends, not from us, and will be the greatest
blow to their efforts to convert the Singhalese into
Christians.

As they walk out of the temple, there are native Singhalese
cheering as the two emerge from inside the temple.

                                        CUT TO:

EXT. OPEN PAVILION ON A COCONUT PLANTATION-- EVENING

A couples weeks later . . .

We see Olcott sitting alone on a chair in the pavilion passing his hands up and down the body of a man, administering magnetic healing. A long line of people waits. HPB walks up to Olcott and taps him on the shoulders.

> HPB
> You are exhausted, Henry. You must stop. In fact the Masters order you to stop before all your vital energy is sapped. You have a long trip back to Bombay tomorrow.

> COLONEL OLCOTT
> You're right. I must stop.

He gets up and signals to the attending monk that he is quitting for the day. The crowd breaks the line and rushes up to him. Some beg him one more healing. But HPB leads him off to their living quarters behind the pavilion.

SOUND: Ringing of Tibetan prayer bowl leads us back to Bombay.

FADE OUT:

INT. THE CROW'S NEST -- DAY

Loud voices in the background in the kitchen. Ms. Bates and Emma Coulomb battling. Olcott and HPB are on the veranda trying to duck the conflict.

> COLONEL OLCOTT
> It's just as I predicted. We've come home to a war. It's all my fault letting that Coulomb woman in charge of the household.

> HPB
> (Fanning herself with a large fan)
> Miss Bates can't keep her mouth shut either. Prattling on like a wild hyena. You know, they didn't talk the whole time we were gone. But listen to them now.

> COLONEL OLCOTT
> Miss Bates doesn't want to relinquish control over this household even if she does nothing most of the day.

> HPB
> Two wild tigresses in a cage. Wimbridge is now in the middle of it from the sound of it. Now it's them two against the Coulombs.

COLONEL OLCOTT
Did you see how they split the servants' quarters in half? Alexis built a wall right down the center of their cottage. Never seen anything like it.

HPB
(Expletives)
How can I get any writing done in this hell?

COLONEL OLCOTT
It's your fault.

HPB
(Expletives)

COLONEL OLCOTT
I'll have to find a situation for Wimbridge. Can't do much for the Coulombs. We can offer Bates her passage back to England.

HPB
Good idea, Moloney. I knew you would find a solution for this one. It would be worth every cent. With all this heat and fighting, I'm feeling fatigued and ill. It's like hell here.
(She fans herself furiously)

COLONEL OLCOTT
We've got to settle this matter once and for all, at least before we travel again. The Sinnetts have invited us to Simla where the Her Majesty's government repairs to cool off in April and May. It should be good for us to contact the powers that be and especially for you, to get out of this heat.

HPB
Master said I should get out of this heat before I get too sick to function. I'm ready to go as soon as you are. By the way, as we got off the carriage in front of the house the other day, I saw that same fellow from the secret service watching us. I think I'll invite him to follow us to Simla.

COLONEL OLCOTT
At least we're safe while he's around. It's like having our own bodyguard. . . that is, unless they throw us both in prison for espionage!

She snaps her fan resolutely back into its folded position and let's out a roar of laughter.

SOUND: Ringing of Tibetan prayer bowl leads us to the cool Hill Station of Simla in the Himalayas.

                                                CUT TO:

EXT. SIMLA PROSPECT HILL -- DAY

ANGLE WIDE

A huge, overweight HPB sits in a sedan chair being carried by eight scrawny Indian coolies up the hill to a picnic area among the majestic Himalayan pines. Following behind are two other sedan chairs bearing Patience Sinnett and MRS. HENDERSON (wife of Major Henderson). The men, Olcott, A.P. Sinnett, MAJOR HENDERSON and another BRITISH OFFICER walk slowly behind the sedan chairs. An entourage of Indian servants bearing baskets of food, blankets and chairs follows.

EXT. SIMLA-PROSPECT HILL--HIMALAYAN WOODS -- DAY

Guests are sitting or milling around the picnic spot. Patience Sinnett is organizing the picnic area with her servants.

                    PATIENCE SINNETT
                (scolding one of the servants)
        We don't have enough tea cups for everyone! There are
        only six sets. Didn't I tell you to add another set
        for Major Henderson's friend?

                    HINDU SERVANT
        All the other tea cups were broken, ma'm.

                    PATIENCE SINNETT
        Why didn't you tell me?

                    MAJOR HENDERSON
        Is there anything I can help you with?

                    PATIENCE SINNETT
        Yes, we're missing a tea cup.

                    MAJOR HENDERSON
        Oh, that must be my fault. I brought the extra person.

                    COLONEL OLCOTT
        I don't mind sharing a tea cup with someone else.

                    MAJOR HENDERSON
        I've got a better idea. Why doesn't Mme. Blavatsky use
        her powers to produce another tea cup set?

We see HPB close her eyes and smile. From her POV, we first see a cluster of scintillating light that transforms itself into a faded and fuzzy image of a cup and saucer. As HPB concentrates on it, the fuzzy image becomes crystal clear at which point another cluster of light carries the image to a tree on the other side of the picnic area and buries it. In the earth under the tree roots, the thought-form of the cup and saucer begin to take on a solid, crystallized form.

> HPB
> (laughing)
> I would need someone strong to dig it up for me.

> MAJOR HENDERSON
> Dig it up?

> HPB
> Because another set is buried under that tree over there.

She points to a tree on the extremity of the picnic area.

> HPB (CONT'D)
> Someone will need a spade to dig through the roots and shrubs. It's under there.

> MAJOR HENDERSON
> (addressing the other British Officer)
> Come on, officer. You're used to improvising. Let's go over and dig.

Everyone follows the two British officers, and they manage to dig with some stone chips and pocket knives.

> BRITISH OFFICER
> Here, I've hit something. Looks like the side of a porcelain cup.

> MAJOR HENDERSON
> Easy now. We don't want to break it. Dig with your hands.

British officer digs carefully like an archaeologist, cutting through tree roots and dusting aside the earth with his bare hands.

> BRITISH OFFICER
> Well, my word! It's a tea cup alright, and a saucer to boot!

> PATIENCE SINNETT
> (running up to the two men)
> I don't believe it! Let me see it. Why, yes, it's identical to my set of tea cups! From the same set!

> A.P. SINNETT
> It's amazing. So this is what you mean by your challenge to both religion and science.

He bows slightly.

> A.P. SINNETT (CONT'D)
> Well done, Madame.

> HPB
> I am glad you see it in that light. Otherwise, how would you explain such a phenomenon? It defies any scientific explanation unless science wants to entertain some occult principles.

> A.P. SINNETT
> How, Madame, I truly wish to understand what we're seeing.

> HPB
> I can only give you a hint. It has to do with controlling, by conscious will, elementals who work with particles of energy. They mould these particles according to the thought-form I give them. It is mind control of the atom particles of matter around us.

> A.P. SINNETT
> Hmmm. This is much too esoteric for my conventional logical brain, I'm afraid. I must reflect and observe more.

Major Henderson approaches HPB and Sinnett beaming from ear to ear.

> MAJOR HENDERSON
> Well, Madame, I am impressed and I would like to join your society. Can you do the paperwork at this moment?

> HPB
> Just look over there in that tree.

Everybody moves toward the tree. The British officer scratches away the underbrush and approaches the tree truck. There, in the V of the first branch is tucked a rolled up document, similar to a diploma.

MAJOR HENDERSON
Well, what do you know! There's a roll of documents.

He steps up to the tree and takes the document. He undoes the ribbon and opens up the diploma.

MAJOR HENDERSON (CONT'D)
It says that I am now a standing member of the Theosophical Society of Simla. Wait, here is a letter tucked inside that goes with it. It's signed by you, Colonel Olcott.

He hands the letter to Olcott.

COLONEL OLCOTT
Well, it's written in my hand. If I hadn't seen it myself I would not have believed it. It's exactly my signature.

MAJOR HENDERSON
This is all very fascinating. I'm certain I can find a scientific reason for all this.

HPB
Be my guest, Major. But don't be too ridiculous in your explanations as we are dealing with something quite sacred whether you see it or not.

Major Henderson half scowls, not knowing how to take HPB's jab.

PATIENCE SINNETT
Let's have supper everyone. And Helena, I have you to thank for keeping this picnic so lively and interesting. Never have we been so blessed with such a . . . well, extraordinary guest!

She turns away and walks back to cluster of servants waiting to start the service. HPB looks sideways to Olcott.

HPB
I'm just like a circus sideshow for these people.

COLONEL OLCOTT
Hush. We're their guests, remember?

FADE OUT:

EXT. SIMLA PROSPECT HILL -- LATER THAT AFTERNOON

Everyone is preparing to break the picnic. The servants are scurrying about gathering and packing things into the picnic hampers. The sedan chair bearers are trying to squeeze HPB back into the sedan chair.

Maj. Henderson walks briskly up to the sedan chair.

> MAJOR HENDERSON
> We've come up with a logical explanation, Madame.

> HPB
> (settling into the sedan chair)
> Let us hear it.

> MAJOR HENDERSON
> A couple hours ago, I was willing to accept all that I saw and experienced. But after thinking further and investigating the circumstances. . . Well, you can see that slope behind the tree over there. Someone could have burrowed a little tunnel from behind the tree and stuck that tea cup and saucer under the ground before we came. In other words, there is some doubt now as to the genuineness of this experiment.

> HPB
> Ridiculous! What more would you have me do?

> MAJOR HENDERSON
> Well, my colleague and I would like you to produce another phenomenon under conditions which we dictate. This way we will be assured of the genuineness of . . .

> HPB
> Major, I give you the prize for the most stupid and absurd explanation. Why and how could the British Army tolerate such stupidity among their ranks? Shame. Get him out of my sight!
> (expletives)

HPB rants and raves at the top of her lungs as the bearers hurriedly carry her away in the sedan chair.

CUT TO:

INT. SINNETT'S HOME IN SIMLA-- BREAKFAST ROOM -- MORNING THE NEXT DAY

In the breakfast room a large window of small paned glass windows in the British style gives out to an exquisite flower garden fenced in by a wall covered with purple bougainvilla. The setting is so English that there is no hint of India, except for the occasional Indian servant who walks in to serve.

                    HPB
          Can you believe that cad yesterday? Such damn nonsense
          coming from a military officer.

                    COLONEL OLCOTT
                (whispering)
          Let's forget it. It's already passed. We're still
          guests here. So, not so loud!

                    HPB
          Don't hush me, Henry. You never stand up for me. That
          goes for yesterday. How could you just stand there
          like a stupid ape and let him insult me with that cock
          and bull story about the tunnel. You've seen enough of
          these phenomena to know they're genuine. You're a real
          coward when it comes to defending the Brotherhood and
          me. You're so afraid of losing your reputation among
          your male peers, even when the facts are right there
          before you.

                    COLONEL OLCOTT
          That's absolutely not true! Hush. They can hear you
          from here.

                    HPB
          Let these idiots listen. It will do them some good.

Sinnett appears in the breakfast room

                    A.P. SINNETT
          Good morning, everyone. That was quite an evening. I
          hope you're not too upset, Helena.

HPB pouting.

                    HPB
          I am. Such stupidity! Or is it plain ignorance?
          While you can sense a principle behind the phenomena,
          the run-of-the-mill develop an insatiable appetite for
          them. One manifestation creates the thirst and blinds

them from searching inward for the principle that made it happen.

                    A.P. SINNETT
          Military men are quite tough to convince, especially
          about things esoteric. So be patient with Major
          Henderson. He means well and is genuinely interested
          in the esoteric.

                    HPB
          It's not toughness. It's pitiful ignorance and
          downright stupidity.

                    A.P. SINNETT
                         (smiling wickedly)
          I don't suspect he'll be coming around anymore while
          you're here.

                    HPB
          Good. I've had enough of such monkeys dressed up in
          the Queen's uniform.

Suddenly a letter-sized paper floats down from the ceiling. Sinnett snatches it in mid-air before it touches the table.

                    A.P. SINNETT
          Now, what is this? Hmmm. It's written in blue ink in
          a very odd pen style. It is addressed to me. But I
          can't read it without my reading glasses. What the?
          Patience! Come quickly.

Patience enters.

                    PATIENCE SINNETT
          What is it, dear?

                    A.P. SINNETT
          Did you just put this on the table for me?

                    HPB
                         (Gritting her teeth)
          Mr. Sinnett! Did you not just witness it falling from
          of the ceiling? We all saw it.

Olcott puts his hand on HPB's arm to calm her.

                    HPB (CONT'D)
          Colonel Olcott and I were sitting here when it
          happened. How could Patience have put it there?

                    A.P. SINNETT
                    (sputtering)
          Ah, yes, Madame. Excuse me. Patience, they are right.
          We were sitting here talking, and this letter just
          floated down from the ceiling.

                    PATIENCE SINNETT
          Dear me. From whom?

                    HPB
          May I look at it?

Sinnett hands the letter to HPB.

                    HPB (CONT'D)
          It's from the Mahatma we work with. It is signed K.H.

                    A.P. SINNETT
          Who is that?

                    COLONEL OLCOTT
          Be honoured, my friend. It is a handwritten letter
          from the Mahatma Koot Houmi or the Master Kuthumi.

                    HPB
          He says this is the first of many contacts he is
          offering you as editor of the most prestigeous
          newspaper in India. He wishes you to think over this
          proposal.

                    A.P. SINNETT
                    (nodding)
          Quite interesting. Quite out of the ordinary, I must
          say. I shall reflect on this proposal and I am
          honored.

The positive energy of the letter lights up the breakfast room, HPB and Olcott bow their heads, and the friction that started the breakfast conversation dissipates. A sense of peace settles over the breakfast room.

                                                  CUT TO:

INT. A.O. HUME'S MANSION ON JAKKO HILL IN SIMLA-- DINING ROOM -- EVENING

Dining room is opulent. Teak Victorian furniture, rose patterned embroidered chairs, chandelier-- Colonial British style.

Table is laid out in the splendour of the rich. Bone china and crystal stemware. White gloved servants are just serving dessert and tea to eleven guests including Olcott, HPB, Mr and Mrs. Hume, and a MRS. GORDON. The Sinnetts are seated at each end of the table.

                    HUME
          That was utterly superb venison. Who hunted it?

                    A.P. SINNETT
          One of the servants. He hunts on his day off.

                    PATIENCE SINNETT
          Does anyone desire more tea? It's Darjeeling tea sent
          here from the Governor in Darjeeling.

                    HPB
               (whispering to Olcott)
          The smell of alcohol and meat fat is making me sick.
          Can you open the window behind you?

Olcott gets up to open the window. A servant rushes up to him to open it for him.

                    PATIENCE SINNETT
          Yes, that's a good idea to open that window. The cool,
          fresh mountain air smells wonderful. With all these
          candles it was getting stuffy in here.

As the room cools down, HPB begins to warm her hands over the candle in front of her.

                    HPB
          Who wants something?

                    MRS. HUME
          Hummm. I do.

                    HPB
          What is it, my dear?

                    MRS. HUME
          If I could really get it back, I should like to have an
          old family jewel that I have not seen for a long time;
          a brooch set round with pearls.

                    HPB
          Have you the image of it clearly in your mind?

> MRS. HUME
> Yes, perfectly clear; strange, it has just come to me in a flash.

HPB looks fixedly at Mrs. Hume for a while, her eyes seeming blank as if looking inward.

> HPB
> It will not be brought into this house but can be found in the garden--I am told by a Brother.

She looks at Mr. Hume directly.

> HPB (CONT'D)
> Do you have a flower-bed shaped like a star?

> MR. HUME
> Why, yes.

HPB stands up and points in a certain direction.

> HPB
> There! In that direction.

> MR. HUME
> Yes, precisely. It's in that direction.

> HPB
> Then, come with me yourself and find it, as I have seen it drop like a point of light in such a bed.

The rest of guests get up to follow HPB, all chatting excitedly. The women put on their wraps, except Mrs. Hume who hesitates to go out into the chilly night air.

> COLONEL OLCOTT
> Friends, before you all go into the garden, if a shadow of doubt hangs over the occurrence, it will be useless for us to go any further.

Those present look questioningly at each other and with one accord agree that everything has been fair and stamped with good faith up this point.

> FADE OUT:

EXT. A.O HUME'S MANSION JAKKO HILLIN SIMLA--GARDEN -- NIGHT

Guests pair up, each pair with a lantern searching through the large star shaped flower bed. Mrs. Hume remains inside standing by the open window and watches the others outside rooting around for the brooch.

                    PATIENCE SINNETT
      Here's something wrapped in a silk handkerchief.

                    COLONEL OLCOTT
      Don't open it. Give it to Mr. Hume.

                    PATIENCE SINNETT
      Humm. There's something hard inside. Here, you are!

Mr. Hume examines the white packet then opens it. He sighs.

                    MR. HUME
        (shouting to his wife who is at the window)
      It's your brooch, dear. It's your long lost brooch. Where did it come from? I'm certain you lost it in England. I know you didn't have it when we came to India.

MR. Hume walks up to the window and hands his wife the brooch.

                    MRS. HUME
      That is right. I lost it before we came here. My God, it IS my long lost brooch.
        (she takes the brooch with tears in her eyes)

                    COLONEL OLCOTT
      Let us go inside and if I may impose upon you all, my friends, I would like to write up an affidavit at this moment-- an account of what happened-- a protocol for our Society, that would be signed by you all as witnesses to this phenomenon. Are you all willing?

A happy murmur filters through the guest, all shaking their heads in agreement.

                                            FADE OUT:

INT. A.O. HUME'S MANSION JAKKO HILL IN SIMLA-- DINING ROOM -- MINUTES LATER

We see Olcott seated at the dining room table with the document he has just drawn up with his pen. Guests line up to sign the document, chatting excitedly about what happened.

INT. A.O. HUME'S MANSION JAKKO HILL IN SIMLA--SMOKING ROOM -- LATER THAT NIGHT

The guests have left and HPB and Olcott have retired upstairs. Hume and Sinnett muse about the evening.

                    A.P. SINNETT
But what do you think of that brooch?

                    MR. HUME
I am certain we didn't have it when we arrived in India. It is the same one my wife lost. However, upon reflection, one can always find a more logical explanation. And it's to those logical explanations that I lean.

                    A.P. SINNETT
You'd better not let Mme. Blavatsky hear that. She's like a firecracker that could go off anytime and anywhere. A savage temper, mind you. I would have thought the Himalayan Mahatmas would have laid their bets on someone more refined, more genteel, more in line with the type of Society they would have to deal with here in India.

                    MR. HUME
And Olcott has much of that untethered American enthusiasm. A bit rough along the edges, I would say, for something as important as this.

                    A.P. SINNETT
Both are quite a pair. Curious they would be chosen for this spiritual endeavour.

                    MR. HUME
Say, I have an idea. Why don't we compose a letter to the Mahatmas--a frank, to-the-point letter, expressing all our doubts and questions would be in order. We can give it to Mme. Blavatsky and ask her to transmit it to them. Then, let's see what happens. Let's see if we get something half intelligent from these fellows. A tea cup out of the ground is fine, but let's see if these highly intelligent supermen can come up with some intelligent teachings.

                    A.P. SINNETT
I'll help you draft something.

                                    FADE OUT:

INT. A.O. HUME'S MANSION JAKKO HILL IN SIMLA-- SMOKING ROOM -- DAY

The following day . . .

                    A.P. SINNETT
She said she sent it.

                    MR. HUME
How did she do it?

                    A.P. SINNETT
She just held it in her hand and looked blankly into space. Then it disappeared.

He snaps his finger.

                    MR. HUME
Then there is something mystical about her even though her manners are atrocious.

                    A.P. SINNETT
She's of the Russian nobility, my friend.

                    MR. HUME
Not a very good representative, I'd say.

                    A.P. SINNETT
    (whispering)
In fact, the Foreign Office paid me a visit when he heard they were coming to visit with us. He said they suspect her of being a Russian spy, especially because they seem to be so close to the natives. I was to report back to them. What do you think?

                    MR. HUME
One never knows. But I find it hard to believe. In fact, someone that emotionally unstable could hardly take the pressures of spy. The more I think of it, the more ridiculous that allegation sounds. . . Wait one second, there's someone at the door.

One of his servants comes to get him.

                  HUME'S SERVANT
Sahib, there's an Indian at the door asking for you.

                    MR. HUME
What the . . .?

EXT. A.O. HUME'S MANSION JAKKO HILL IN SIMLA--FRONT DOOR -- DAY

Hume approaches the door and sees a ragged, dirty Indian messenger. He motions his servant to take the letter from the Indian. On Hume's face is the look of disdain and disgust at the Indian. After the servant takes the letter, Hume backs off, nods his head to the Indian, and motions his servant to shut the door in the Indian's face.

INT. A.O. HUME'S MANSION JAKKO HILL IN SIMLA-- SMOKING ROOM -- DAY

                    MR. HUME
     Some street urchin delivered this envelope. He was reeking. Who in the world could it be from?

He rips open the envelope and takes out a letter.

                    MR. HUME (CONT'D)
     Well, well, well, it's from one of Madame's Mahatmas, the one who signs himself K.H. That was quick. Let's see what he says. Hmmm. You can read the rest later, but here's what he says about Blavatsky.

MASTER KOOT HOUMI (V.O.)
I am painfully aware of the fact that the habitual incoherence of her statements--especially when excited--and her strange ways make her in your opinion a very undesirable transmitter of our teachings. Nevertheless, kind Brothers, this unbalanced mind, the seeming incongruity of her speeches and ideas, her nervous excitement, all that, in short, which is so calculated to upset the feelings of sober-minded people, whose notions of reserve and manners are shocked by such strange outbursts of what they regard as her temper . . . is intimately connected with her occult training in Tibet, and due to her being sent out alone into the world to gradually prepare the way for others. After nearly a century of fruitless search, our chiefs had to avail themselves of the only opportunity to send out a European body upon European soil to serve as a connecting link between that country and our own. Remember she tried to explain the seven principles of the human being. Now no man or woman unless he be an initiate of the "fifth circle", can leave the precincts of Bod-Las or Tibet as you know it and return back into the world in his integral whole. One at least of his seven satellites has to remain behind for two reasons: the first to form the necessary connecting link, the wire of transmission-- the second as the safest warrantor that certain things will never be divulged. She is no exception to the rule. So to hold her responsible for her purely physiological excitement and to let her see your contemptuous smiles was positively cruel.

They both lean back in their chairs in silence. A few seconds later

A.P. SINNETT
Well, I guess our suggestion that they replace this pair was not taken very well.

MR. HUME
No. However, one thing is for sure, this is quite an erudite Indian. I guess we've both been heartily rebuked. What do you say, my friend? Another scotch?

A.P. SINNETT
Yes, with pleasure. No doubt we are being watched. I wonder what they must think about strong drink. Have you noticed that neither HPB nor Olcott drink? The Mahatma's explanation about HPB will change the way I look at her from now on.

MR. HUME
I hope that will appease the Mahatmas. My, he was quite adamant. Yet, I'm sure we can harbour our own opinions about matters and people and not be forced to conform to some mythical Himalayan super-man.

A.P. SINNETT
Does that rankle you?

MR. HUME
Coming from where it does, yes, frankly.

A.P. SINNETT
Let's put our personal prejudices aside, my friend. We may be dealing with the supernatural. Maybe we have opened up a dialogue with this Mahatma.

MR. HUME
I still say we do not really know where these letters are originating. So let's not jump to any conclusions that this letter comes from a supernatural. For all we know, it could be Mme Blavatsky herself making them up.

A.P. SINNETT
By the way, they're leaving shortly on a tour of the plains.

A.O. HUME
Humm. Can't help thinking this whole thing is a ruse of some sort. With them gone, we can think through things a bit better.

CUT TO:

INT. BRITISH RAJ FOREIGN OFFICE IN SIMLA -- MORNING

Colonel Olcott is seated before an ornate desk of a high level British Officer of the Foreign Department in their summer office in Simla.

BRITISH OFFICIAL OF FOREIGN OFFICE

Well, my Colonel, your partner, Mme Blavatsky, is the talk of this little town. Our friend, Mr. Hume, said you have an important matter to discuss with this office.

COLONEL OLCOTT
Yes, thank you for consenting to see me this morning.First, here is a letter of introduction from

the Secretary of State in America which I filed with the British government in Bombay. Second, here are naturalization papers of Mme. Blavatsky that make her an American citizen.

> BRITISH OFFICIAL OF FOREIGN OFFICE

Yes, yes very impressive. What can I do for you?

> COLONEL OLCOTT

False reports, based upon ignorance or malice, that my colleague and I are Russian spies, have placed us under government surveillance. Are you aware of this?

> BRITISH OFFICIAL OF FOREIGN OFFICE

Not at this moment. Please go on.

> COLONEL OLCOTT

The surveillance has been quite blatant and ,if you wish, clumsily executed so as to make clear to anyone who chooses to associate with us that they would incur the displeasure of high officials.

> BRITISH OFFICIAL OF FOREIGN OFFICE

Oh, my Colonel. I am sure this was not the intention of the security forces. They are just executing prudence toward westerners who mix with the natives. We must ascertain if there is any ulterior political agenda that might endanger Her Majesty's government in India.

> COLONEL OLCOTT

Please be assured, sir, that our presence in India has no political aims. We are here primarily to educate those we meet about the works and presence of the Trans-himalayan Brotherhood.

> BRITISH OFFICIAL OF FOREIGN OFFICE

Ahem! Yes, indeed. I can see that. Right. I mean . . . let us do the following. I shall issue an order to the security services to cease any further surveillance.

> COLONEL OLCOTT

That would be wonderful. That we will no longer be followed throughout India?

The official stands up. Olcott follows.

> BRITISH OFFICIAL OF FOREIGN OFFICE
> Yes, I guarantee it. And on behalf of Her Majesty, I welcome you officially to the Great Empire of British India.

> COLONEL OLCOTT
> And on behalf of Mme. Blavatsky and myself, we accept this generous welcome.

SOUND: Ringing of Tibetan prayer bowl leads us to the suffocatingly hot plains of India.

> FADE OUT:

INT. INDIAN TRAIN TRAVELING FROM SIMLA TO THE PLAINS-- DAY

We see Olcott and HPB sitting in a crowded train. The breeze coming through the open train windows is like a blast furnace and HPB looks withered and is barely hanging on. They are the only white people riding in common class. Pregnant mother, screaming kids, loud talking men, on board hawkers shouting. A GROUP OF KIDS gather to stare at this strange couple.

> HPB
> (forgetting the heat and smiling)
>
> What's that?

She causes bells to tinkle above the kids' heads.

GROUP OF KIDS shriek with laughter and try to catch the sounds.

Suddenly a sealed letter drops from the ceiling of the train carriage. The kids point to the letter drifting down and try to snatch it, but Olcott reaches out and gets it first

> COLONEL OLCOTT
> (looking at the letter)
> What's this?

> HPB
> It's from the Master Kuthumi. He wants met to transmit it to the Sinnett.

> COLONEL OLCOTT
> Can we read it first?

> HPB
> It's sealed, which means it's for his eyes only.

HPB takes the letter from Olcott, holds it between her palms and takes a deep breath. The letter vanishes from her hands, while the kids watch in wonderment exclaiming in Hindi what happened.

> HPB (CONT'D)
> There! It's done!

We see the back of the train as it pushes eastward toward Benares.

CUT TO:

INT. A.O. HUME'S MANSION JAKKO HILLIN SIMLA--SMOKING ROOM -- EVENING

Sinnett is sitting in a plush library of Hume's home in Simla. Hume is standing with a decanter of whiskey in his hand.

> A.O. HUME
> Add a little more to your nightcap, old chap.

> A.P SINNETT
> Right so. This cigar is superb. Where did you get it?

> A.O. HUME
> It came all the way from Cuba. I keep this special box for friends who appreciate fine cigars.

> A.P SINNETT
> So what's on your mind? When your boy servant gave me your note, I came as soon as possible.

> A.O. HUME
> I just thought that now the two have left, we can speak of certain matters privately.

> A.P SINNETT
> Precisely. I had the same thought and wanted to talk to you, too.

> A.O. HUME
> Colonel Olcott mentioned that a few erudite Anglo-Indians here in Simla would like to form a chapter of the Theosophical Society here.

> A.P. SINNETT
> I see our thoughts are running in the same direction. It was precisely this matter I wanted to discuss with you, too. If such a society were to be established, to whom would we answer administratively?

                    A.O. HUME
I suppose to Colonel Olcott who is the President of the
Theosophical Society.

                    A.P SINNETT
What do you think of him?

                    A.O. HUME
A credulous fool but undeniably an honest man.

                    A.P. SINNETT
If such a society were formed here, undoubtably we
would be in a position to be its officers.

                    A.O. HUME
Given our present close contact with the "Theosophical
Twins", I would say yes.

                    A.P. SINNETT
But what rankles me a bit is that we would just be a
branch.

He stops to clip his cigar.

                    A.O. HUME
What is on your mind, old chap?

                    A.P. SINNETT
I'm a bit concerned about the Colonel, frankly. He
belongs more in the wild west than in polite "society".
Granted, we have to rely on the ole lady to give us a
show from time to time, but what can the Colonel do
that we can't?

                    A.O. HUME
Good question.

                    A.P. SINNETT
Our Anglo-Indian friends might be offended by his . . .
well, abrupt and rather crude manner. Metaphysics is
so delicate at times. Besides, I don't want to be in
position where I must answer to Olcott. There! I said
it.

                    A.O. HUME
And if the Mahatmas are willing to send us their
teachings, why do we need to answer to them at all?

                    A.P. SINNETT
Right. That's what I've been thinking also. We
wouldn't want to undermine their Theosophical Society,
but we could have our own independent society here in
Simla. If we manage to strike up an exchange with the
so-called Mahatmas we could disseminate the teachings
ourselves. With my newspaper, I am prepared to do
this. Separate but equal, I say.

                    A.O. HUME
Precisely. But now that we're speaking frankly, there
is another thing that bothers me. It is the way they
so easily rub elbows with the natives.

                    A.P. SINNETT
Yes, this is a bit disconcerting. It could be their
American nature, you know, "everyone is equal".

                    A.O. HUME
    (smiling wryly))
As long as they're not negro.

                    A.P. SINNETT
True, true. I wonder if the Mahatmas would go along
with this plan?

At that moment the sealed letter that HPB had transmitted from the
train drifts down from the ceiling of Sinnett's library.

                    A.P. SINNETT (CONT'D)
Well, well. What have we here?

He picks up the letter from the floor, searches in his desk drawer
for a letter opener, and gingerly slices open the envelope.

                    KUTHUMI (V.O.)
Anticipating the gist of your conversation well in
advance of it happening, I take this opportunity to set
the record straight. Mme. B and Mr. O . . . of these
two persons one has already given three-fourths of a
life, the other six years of manhood's prime to us, and
both will so labour to the close of their days. Would
it not be palpable injustice to ignore them as you have
both proposed in an important field of Theosophical
effort? Neither of them has the least desire to
interfere with the management of the contemplated
Anglo-Indian Branch. But, the new society, if formed
at all, must be, in fact, a Branch of the Parent body.

                    A.O. HUME
          Is that all?

                    A.P. SINNETT
               (looking a bit stunned and sheepish at the same
                 time)
          There are a few other paragraphs concerning other
          matters. But I am baffled at the timing of this
          letter. Could they be so advanced that they can even
          anticipate the conclusion of a future conversation?

                    A.O. HUME
          Remarkable for their race. I should think if they were
          real, they could at least appear in person so we could
          discuss this matter man-to-man, so to speak.

                    A.P. SINNETT
          I agree, rather than a bossy directive. If we could
          just see them with our own two eyes, these letters
          would have more credibility.

At this instant the Master Kuthumi appears in his astral body and stands directly in front of the two as they speak. We see the back of his form. But neither Hume nor Sinnett are able to see the Master.

                    A.O. HUME
          I agree, but that letter did drop from the ceiling.
          And Mme Blavatsky is far from here. So who did it?

                    A.P. SINNETT
          If these Masters do exist, a letter drifting down from
          the ceiling is not enough. They must show us more
          convincing proof of their existence.

The Master Kuthumi's astral body fades out.

                                                       CUT TO:

EXT. INDIAN TRAIN STATION -- NOON

The steam train taking HPB and Olcott to Benares chugs into a station. Both HPB and Olcott asleep upright on their train carriage bench. The same scene of chaos as new passengers pile on the moving train and train passengers try to alight. In a section on the platform reserved for white people, a group of well-wishers waits on the platform with garlands of flowers. As Olcott and HPB struggle off the train, the well-wishers advance toward them and drape garlands over them.

> WELL-WISHER MAN #1
> We came, all of us, hoping to get a glimpse of you two.

> WELL-WISHER WOMAN #2
> Can you show us something special, Madame? Your fame has reached even this small town.

HPB smiles and causes Tibetan bells to tinkle above their heads. The women break out in laughter, covering their faces with their sari trains.

> COLONEL OLCOTT
> Here, sir, I have everything prepared. How many of you will constitute this branch?

> WELL-WISHER MAN #1
> (smiling broadly and shaking his head, Indian style)
> All ten of us.

> COLONEL OLCOTT
> Good. Raise your right hand. I agree to uphold the bylaws of the Theosophical Society and vow to spread brotherhood among mankind.

> GROUP OF TEN
> (repeats the oath)
> The train whistle blows.

> COLONEL OLCOTT
> Oh, it is already time for us to get back on the train.

HPB and Olcott struggle back onto the crowded train.

INT. INDIAN TRAIN -- AFTERNOON

HPB and Olcott force their way through the packed train carriage to retake their seats. The group of kids on the train have saved seats on the bench opposite one another. Olcott and HPB sink into their seats, Olcott resting his arm on the train window sill.

> HPB
> I have something important to convey to you.

> COLONEL OLCOTT
> Later. With this heat and noise in the carriage, I cannot concentrate.

Camera focuses on HPB as she puts her hand gently on Olcott's arm. Suddenly the whole crowd on their carriage freezes as if in suspended animation and time. We hear the last of the train whistle as it gets cut short. In this split second of time, HPB states her thoughts to Olcott while everything around them is frozen.

                        HPB
Have you met those new theosophists before?

                    COLONEL OLCOTT
Why, yes. I think they were from the Arya Samaj group.

                        HPB
If you're not sure, how could you have formed them into a branch society? They know nothing about Theosophy.

                    COLONEL OLCOTT
But that's why I did it. You have willing people who are open to what we have to say. Now, all we must do is keep sending them the Theosophist, and they will learn.

                        HPB
I wonder what their true motives are for wanting to associate with us. It's certainly not a thirst to know the spiritual laws that drives them, for they don't even know what we're teaching.

                    COLONEL OLCOTT
How can they find out if without our society?

                        HPB
Remember when we first met? How you thirsted for this knowledge! That's whom we should be entertaining. Look at Damodar. He hungers for the truth so much that he's willing to give up caste and inheritance and bear his father's wrath.

                    COLONEL OLCOTT
These are few and far between, so we must be willing to feed the truth to anyone who is willing to listen.

                        HPB
I keep wondering, Moloney, if it's because we're white foreigners, and they think they can gain some advantage from adhering to the society. Like Hurrychund, for instance.

                    COLONEL OLCOTT
          Maybe their motives are not that selfish. Perhaps our
          ideas give them more pride for their own Hindu or
          Buddhist religions.

                    HPB
          Perhaps. But maybe we should be more mindful of the
          people we accept into the society, Moloney. We're here
          to spread theosophical ideas not to build an
          organization.

                    COLONEL OLCOTT
          But an organization is essential to spread these ideas.

                    HPB
          I agree somewhat but these powerful ideas have a way of
          spreading much faster through the minds of people and
          other channels of thinking . . . more than you realize,
          ole chum.

                    COLONEL OLCOTT
          But without the Theosophical Society do you think we
          can accomplish this?

                    HPB
          Of course not. But I don't think forming branches so
          hastily just so that we can claim a large following is
          a good idea. The Masters caution us on this point. We
          must simply make ourselves and the Masters' teachings
          available to those who hunger for the truth, that's
          all.

                    COLONEL OLCOTT
          We must take advantage of this enthusiasm, not
          discourage it.

                    HPB
          Enthusiasm is not always wisdom. It can be a trap.

HPB gently lifts her hand from Olcott's arm and the whole train car
comes back to life. The train whistle picks up from where it left
off.

EXT. INDIAN TRAIN -- DAY

The next day the train continues to wend its way east through the
flat, hot plains of India.

                                                  CUT TO:

EXT. BENARES TRAIN STATION -- DAY

The following day . . .

Train chugs into Benares station teeming with people. It is hot like a furnace. Among the hordes of people on the platform is a group of Indians dressed in western attire waiting in the area roped off for white people. They look more intellectual as they are from the Benares College. Spotting HPB and Olcott, hot and exhausted, they quickly rush toward them and drape flower garlands around them.

                              CUT TO:

INT. BENARES COLLEGE HALL-- EVENING

We join Damodar, HPB, Olcott, Dr. G. THIBAULT, President of Benares College, and several other pundits who have gathered to discuss the subject of Yoga.

Sitting at the edge of chair DR. G. THIBAULT, frock-coat buttoned to his chin, his intellectual pale face as if pronouncing a funeral oration, short hair standing in spikes on his head, begins.

                    DR. THIBAULT
               (Thick German accent)
          Madame Blavatsky, these Pundits tell me that
          undoubtedly in the ancient times, there were Yogis who
          had actually developed the Siddhis described in the
          Shastras; that they could do wonderful things; for
          instance, they could make fall in a room like this, a
          shower of roses; but now nobody can do that.

                    HPB
          Oh, they say that, do they? They say no one can do it
          now? Well, I'll show them; and you may tell them from
          me that if the modern Hindus were less sycophantic to
          the British, less in love with their vices, and more
          like their ancestors in many ways they would not have
          to make such a humiliating confession, nor get an old
          Western hippopotamus of woman to prove the truth of
          their Shastras!

HPB sits with her lips together. She mutters a secret mantra. We see her visualize the thought-form "Long-stem red roses". She then sweeps her right hand through the air with an imperious gesture, and atomic particles gather together and engulf the thought-form. With another wave of the hand, dozens of roses materialize and fall from the ceiling onto the heads of the group.

There is a momentary shock, then people scramble for the roses. Dr. Thibault does not move but remains ramrod stiff trying to figure out what just happened.

>   DR. THIBAULT
>   Ah, so. I will have many questions for you.

>   FADE OUT:

FADE IN:

INT. BENARES COLLEGE HALL -- EVENING

>   DR. THIBAULT
>   (Thick German accent)
>   I have some questions about the Sankhya philosophy. It
>   is behind the roses you created this afternoon, no?

>   HPB
>   Yes.

>   DR. THIBAULT
>   Ah so. It is under the fifth principle of Sankhya that
>   you did this, no?

>   HPB
>   Precisely, professor.

>   DR. THIBAULT
>   What else is associated with fifth power of the soul?

>   HPB
>   The ability to predict future events, understand
>   unknown languages, cure diseases, divine unexpressed
>   thoughts, and understand the language of the heart.

>   DR. THIBAULT
>   Ah so. Is every soul capable of this?

>   HPB
>   Yes.

>   DR. THIBAULT
>   I see. Can my soul one day do all this?

>   HPB
>   Of course.

DR. THIBAULT
How did you come to know all this?

HPB
Sankhya represents an outward manifestion of deep occult truths that underlie all religions, even Christianity.

DR. THIBAULT
But how could Christianity be remotely connected to Sankya?

HPB
It is. The symbols and icons of all the major religions of the world point to the same principles and cosmic laws.

DR. THIBAULT
Where can you learn these secrets?

HPB
I need only understand these laws, and I can perform the same manifestations as your Sankhya yogis. Then follow the straight and narrow path of initiation that the Trans-Himalayan Brotherhood has made available to mankind.

DR. THIBAULT
Are you an initiate on this path?

HPB
What do you think?

DR. THIBAULT
Indeed you must be, Madame, if you can answer my questions about Sankya without having specifically studied it.

HPB
Is there anything else?

DR. THIBAULT
Yes, as you see, everybody got a rose but me. As a souvenir of this very delightful evening, could you . . .

HPB
. . Oh, yes, certainly, as many as you like.

Again HPB mutters something and sweeps her hand through the air and more roses fall. This time, one hits Dr. Thibault on his head and lands in his lap while he sits ramrod straight showing no emotions or reaction to what has befallen him.

Olcott bursts into laughter.

                    DR. THIBAULT
    The weight multiplied by the velocity proves that is must have come from a great distance.

A speck of a smile comes over the professor's face as he turns toward HPB and stretches out his hand for a handshake.

                                    CUT TO:

INT. INDIAN TRAIN -- AFTERNOON

Indian train ploughs through countryside. HPB and Olcott on board reading, fanning, sleeping . . .

SOUND: Ringing of Tibetan prayer bowl leads to South India, the Buckingham Canal.

                                    CUT TO:

EXT. BUCKINGHAM CANAL -- MORNING

South of Nellore India. The huge hulk of HPB sitting in a sedan chair being carried by six bearers negotiating their way down a rocky slope to the Buckingham Canal. Colonel Olcott and others follow in their sedan chairs with four bearers each picking their way down the rocky path.

One of the bearers shouts in Tamil

                      BEARER
      (pointing excitedly)
    There's the canal.

                      HPB
    Thank God. Fifteen miles thrown from side to side on these rocks is enough!

                  COLONEL OLCOTT
    Think of the poor bearers under you!

                    HPB
    Why, you ---expletives

> COLONEL OLCOTT
> (laughing)

FADE OUT:

INT. HOUSEBOAT ON THE BUCKINGHAM CANAL NEAR MADRAS -- EVENING

> COLONEL OLCOTT
> Everywhere we've gone, the crowds have been unrelenting. Finally, let's have some peace and quiet.

> HPB
> The heat this afternoon was unbearable. I don't know how you manage to stand up there and address the masses with that long beard of yours. I almost fainted. . . . Ah, did you just feel that?

> COLONEL OLCOTT
> That must be a gust of the monsoon winds picking up. I feel the boat moving now; must have filled the sails. Let's go outside.

EXT. ON TOP THE HOUSEBOAT -- EVENING

HPB and Olcott crawl out of their cabin and sit on the roof of the low lying houseboat. The now steady breeze fans them under a full moon.

> HPB
> Look how the moonlight reflects off the water. This is the first moment of quiet we've had in weeks. Listen to the waves lapping against the boat. What more could we ask for?
>   (Silence for a couple seconds)
> Any regrets, Moloney, getting involved with me and the Mahatmas?

> COLONEL OLCOTT
> Not one ounce! I'd give my life a thousand times over to do this.

> HPB
> They chose you well. We've been at this a lot longer than you suspect.

> COLONEL OLCOTT
> I suspect a few lifetimes, eh?

HPB
More than a few. . . I've been thinking. Who among the thousands we've encountered would you consider were like you a few years back?

COLONEL OLCOTT
Hmmm. That's a good question. Not many. Perhaps Damodar. I had thought the Swami could have been a true adept, but we were sorely disappointed.

HPB
Look how many phenomena I've been allowed to produce at the expense of my health. Just to shake up hard-headed human logic and give them something to question the infallibility of either science or theology. A very simple strategy the Mahatmas created. Allow people to question.

COLONEL OLCOTT
I think you've achieved that, old chum. People are questioning, perhaps within.

HPB
Are they really? I've noticed more their unquenchable thirst for phenomena. One exhibit won't satisfy and I think if I did one hundred, it still wouldn't satisfy. Do these people really understand what they are looking at?

COLONEL OLCOTT
Truthfully, I don't think so. If you want my honest opinion, I think the more you do, the more it looks like a circus rather than a tool to shock them into thinking esoterically. Really.

HPB
Moloney, that's exactly the conclusion I've come to. They're thrilled at first, then the scepticism and the attacks, and then the stubborn mule comes out in all of them.

COLONEL OLCOTT
You know why? Because if they believed the phenomena were genuine, they would have to change their whole way of thinking. This is too big a price to pay.

HPB
Right! The human mind is the most difficult thing to change on this earth. Buddha, Jesus, Mohammed, and all the avatars after them. How they tried!

COLONEL OLCOTT
But the Theosophical Society continues to grow. We've added many branches on this trip through India. Then we have the New York, London and Corfu branches--all inert though. You and I are not exactly spring chickens. How are we to expand this society?

HPB
All I hope to do is color modern thinking with theosophical ideas rather than extend the society throughout the world.

COLONEL OLCOTT
That was our original idea when we first came here, but could you have guessed there would be so much interest among the Indians?

HPB
Do not fool yourself, friend. Many are the motives for joining this society, the least of which is the occult angle.

COLONEL OLCOTT
Honestly, deep down I must agree with you. Our society is conceived as a white man's spiritual group that is very sympathetic with the Asian religions. And perhaps 90% of our members have personal and selfish reasons to benefit from associating with us.

HPB
Those who oppose us outright, like the Christian missionaries, are really more honest in that respect.

COLONEL OLCOTT
So where should we go from here? We can't give up.

HPB
I think the Mahatmas underestimated the underlying darkness we would encounter. Yes, yes, we are received with great enthusiasm, draped with garlands of flowers, hosted by Maharajahs and princes, but all for naught if we consider our occult goals. I posed this question to the Boss.

COLONEL OLCOTT
And what did he say?

                    HPB
It would take decades, if not centuries to pull mankind out of this present state of thinking, save a few here and there.

                    COLONEL OLCOTT
So should we give up?

                    HPB
Forge forth, nonetheless, the Boss says. I have a very important book to write--the follow-on to ISIS. This one, I will leave for the generations to come.

                    COLONEL OLCOTT
Then you must concentrate on that book from hereon. I'll do the traveling.

                    HPB
In the meantime, we can promote universal brotherhood. It sounds grand but I think most can understand what it means on many levels.

                    COLONEL OLCOTT
Brotherhood. This is something people would understand. If we can at least introduce to the world that all religions and science come from the same Source.

                    HPB
. . . then perhaps we can sow the seeds of Brotherhood worldwide.

                    COLONEL OLCOTT
Ah, yes. So we promote Brotherhood based on the inextricable proof that all religion and knowledge come from the same Source, therefore there are no divisions, no separation, just different sides of the same coin.

                    HPB
In a nutshell, Moloney, you've got it. It sounds simple, doesn't it?

                    COLONEL OLCOTT
What about the occult mysteries?

                    HPB
We shall continue this track because it underlies all
what we do. It will remain the backbone of the
society, but discretely and in relative secrecy. Those
who thirst for the fount may come. Those who are
satisfied with Brotherhood, let them practice it and
make a better world.

                    COLONEL OLCOTT
Well at least the latter would not force people to
revolutionize their lives. Such as Damodar had to. .
. giving up caste, inheritance, and marriage to pursue
the occult route.

                    HPB
Exactly.

                    COLONEL OLCOTT
So from hereon we reorient the whole Theosophical
Society on the roof of this humble houseboat, floating
down the Buckingham canal in India?

                    HPB
And we're not alone, either.

We see the sails of the houseboat fill with the monsoon winds and the houseboat glides down the canal.

SOUND: Ringing of Tibetan prayer bowl leads us to the city of Madras.

                                        CUT TO:

EXT. OUTSIDE MADRAS -- MORNING

A horse-drawn carriage heading down the coast outside of Madras with Colonel Olcott, HPB and an INDIAN BUSINESSMAN. Colonel Olcott and the INDIAN BUSINESSMAN seated on back bench of carriage, HPB sits on front bench facing them. .

EXT. CARRIAGE OUTSIDE OF MADRAS-- FAVOR BACK BENCH OF CARRIAGE -- MORNING

                    INDIAN BUSINESSMAN
You must see this property. It is perfect for you and
your organization. Very cheap. The owner wants to get
rid of it as fast as possible.

                    COLONEL OLCOTT
Why is that?

INDIAN BUSINESSMAN
The train now goes very close to Ooty in the Ghats and like so many high officials, he now prefers the cool mountain air to the hot humid seaside.

COLONEL OLCOTT
We have been offered many properties around India, but we will know the right one when we see it. We never thought of Madras had it not been for our good friend T. Subba Row who suggested it.

INDIAN BUSINESSMAN
I am sure you will love this place. It is perfect.

EXT. CARRIAGE OUTSIDE MADRAS--MOVING DOWN DIRT ROAD -- MORNING

Carriage turns off the main road and heads down a dirt path toward the sea. The small road bordered on both sides by enormous tropical trees and plants.

INDIAN BUSINESSMAN
Come. That beautiful palatial building in the front of us used to serve as a country palace for a very rich man and his family. There are some riverside bungalows, stables, go-downs, and a very pleasant swimming bath area near the ocean.

HPB
It's stunning. I love it. Moloney, look at those huge mango and banyan trees. This is like paradise.

COLONEL OLCOTT
It is paradise. What do you think HPB?

HPB
No doubt. This is the future home of the Theosophical Society.

INDIAN BUSINESSMAN
Because the owner is very much aware of you both and your work, he will let you have this property for 9000 rupees. It's a nominal sum as you can see.

COLONEL OLCOTT
Sold. We'll find the money somehow. Will the owner allow us to pay him over time?

INDIAN BUSINESSMAN
I am certain he can trust you.

COLONEL OLCOTT
Well, chum, we must go back to Bombay and pack up everything. When is this property available?

INDIAN BUSINESSMAN
Immediately.

COLONEL OLCOTT
We need a few months to arrange everything. Perhaps toward the end of this year?

INDIAN BUSINESSMAN
We will be expecting you.

SOUND: Ringing of Tibetan prayer bowl takes us back to Bombay

CUT TO:

INT. COULOMB QUARTERS IN THE CROW'S NEST--NIGHT

EMMA COULOMB
The boss told me to start packing up things. It appears they've bought a palace in Madras. I told you there's more money than appears.

ALEXIS COULOMB
You were right about the money. This old house is just a cover.

EMMA COULOMB
Didn't I tell you? They visit Maharajas and Maharanis all over India. They know the ones with the money.

ALEXIS COULOMB
What kind of place is this in Madras?

EMMA COULOMB
A palace. I heard them talking. Near the beach. Huge park area. Massive trees. I can picture it. Belonged to a big cat in the Indian government. I think we're going to be very happy there, Alexis.

ALEXIS COULOMB
If it's a big place that means more work.

EMMA COULOMB
Think of the rich and powerful who will pass through that palace. Surely one will take us in and make us happy. Olcott and Blavatsky are too stingy.

> Everything goes to the society. We'd never get enough money to get the hell out of here from them.

ALEXIS COULOMB
> You're right as always, Emma.

EMMA COULOMB
> I'm just as good a medium as HPB. Only she don't know it. But I can see us sitting on a pile of gold.

EXT. THE CROW'S NEST -- MORNING

Two months later . . .

HPB and Olcott sit on the veranda taking their breakfast

HPB
> Last night I received a message from the Boss. He said you should not go back to Ceylon. We should proceed to Adyar instead.

COLONEL OLCOTT
> How could that be? My work there is going so well, and I've finally got the whole Buddhist education project going again.

HPB
> You shouldn't go back there. There's too much to do here. I agree with them.

COLONEL OLCOTT
> Nonsense. I cannot back out now. I'm too committed to the kind souls of Buddhists there.

HPB
> That is the problem, Moloney. Your personal ego is too much involved, and it's leading you off the narrow path of our mission.

COLONEL OLCOTT
> But I've promised them and I won't break my promises.

HPB
> Then I order you not to go back there. Don't you do the Masters' bidding?

COLONEL OLCOTT
Or your own personal bidding? One day it's this and one day it's that. How can I be sure? I'm sure they wouldn't want me to break my promises. Restoring Buddhism in the schools. Can't you see that's in line with the Masters' bidding?

HPB
We should be neutral and not promote any one religion, in this case Buddhism, over the other.

COLONEL OLCOTT
Do you agree we should let the Christian missionaries desecrate the tradition of Buddhism in Ceylon?

HPB
Of course not. But promoting Buddhism is not the goal of the Theosophical Society. The Buddhist leaders in Ceylon should bear that burden, not the Theosophical Society.

COLONEL OLCOTT
I'm going nonetheless.

HPB
Then I'll have nothing to do with you from now on.

She gets up and stalks off to her bedroom slamming the door behind her. Olcott rolls a cigarette, shaking his head. Then HPB storms out to the veranda.

HPB (CONT'D)
Here, this is what the Mahatmas dictated to me last night. Clearly, They do not want you to spend so much time in Ceylon.

COLONEL OLCOTT
Then you've been listening to the wrong voices, HPB. The wrong voices . . .

She storms back into the house and slams the door to her bedroom.

INT. THE CROW'S NEST -- MORNING ONE WEEK LATER

HPB joins Colonel Olcott on the veranda

COLONEL OLCOTT
I was afraid I would have to leave without seeing you. You've been sulking in your room for over a week now.

                    HPB
I've been writing. I've started that book the Masters
want me to write. I hope you have a fruitful trip.
All I've done is convey to what the Masters want us to
do. You can do as you please. They never force you.
I have my own agenda.

                    COLONEL OLCOTT
What do you mean?

                    HPB
The boss has called me to Darjeeling in the Himalayas.
I am slowly dying in this heat. I won't have much time
left on earth. Look at my legs. How they have
swollen!

                    COLONEL OLCOTT
My god! Have you seen the Doctor?

                    HPB
How could I? Barred up in that room.

                    COLONEL OLCOTT
That was your own choice. What did Doctor Dudley say?

                    HPB
I told him my blood is transformed into water. The
heat and humidity of Bombay are unbearable. I told him
I may die any moment as a result of excitement.

                    COLONEL OLCOTT
Are you trying another tactic to stop me from going to
Ceylon?

                    HPB
Go your way, Moloney. I'll do the Masters' bidding.
You can do yours.

                    COLONEL OLCOTT
                    (Shouting)
I AM doing the Masters' bidding!

                    HPB
You only think you are. Anyway, do as you please.
I'll take Mohini and Babula with me. Mohini will
contact all the TS branches on the way. I'll meet with
all of them and teach whatever needs to be taught.

                    COLONEL OLCOTT
Do you think I'll be twiddling my thumbs in Ceylon?

                    HPB
          As I said, you do as you please. I've merely conveyed
          the message to you.

                    COLONEL OLCOTT
                (Big sigh)

SOUND: Ringing of Tibetan prayer bowl

                                        CUT TO:

EXT. "TOY" STEAM TRAIN HIMALAYAS TO DARJEELING END OF SEPTEMBER,
1882 -- AFTERNOON

Famous "Toy" train makes its way slowly up the mountain on the way
to Darjeeling. It is filled with British government staff and
well-dressed wives.

EXT. TRAIN STATION IN DARJEELING HIMALAYAS -- EVENING

WIDE ANGLE: White carriage with white horses waits at station and
we see HPB from a distance get off the train and walk straight to
carriage. A filmy form of the Master Morya awaits her. They drive
off into the mist that is beginning to settle on this hill station.

INT. BACK CHAMBER IN A HIMALAYAN BUDDHIST TEMPLE-- THAT EVENING

HPB is lying on a wooden bed gasping for breath.

                    MORYA
          The air is very thin here in the Himalayas.

He passes his hand over HPB. Her breathing returns to normal

                    HPB
          I am dying, Master. The long journey here, the heat of
          the plains, I cannot last long.

                    MORYA
          We will restore you. Your mission is not finished . .
          . unless you wish to end it now.

                    HPB
          If you can restore me body, then I wish to continue
          until I have finished.

> MORYA
> Rest in this room for a few days. The nuns from the neighbouring convent will care for you but Kuthumi and I will use whatever power we have to restore you.

> HPB
> I am grateful, dear Master.

> MORYA
> We are grateful for one such as you. You cannot know how grateful. Suffer no more.

He passes his hand over her body and she falls into a deep sleep.

SOUND: Ringing of Tibetan prayer bowl

CUT TO:

INT. ADYAR-MADRAS HEADQUARTERS UPSTAIRS HALLWAY -- AFTERNOON

Several months later . . . Emma Coulomb creeps as quietly as possible down the hallway carrying a tray of tea.

> HPB
> Stop that noise! I'm writing and can't concentrate with all the noise you're making outside there!

HPB swings open the door of her bedroom.

> HPB (CONT'D)
> Oh, it's you. You're making too much noise, Emma! Stop it! My nerves are on fire, can't you see?

> EMMA COULOMB
> But Madame, I've brought your tea.

> HPB
> Put it there and let me be!

> EMMA COULOMB
> I must speak to you about something very important.

> HPB
> I don't have time. Can't you see I'm busy?

> EMMA COULOMB
> It is very important.

                    HPB
          Come in, then.

INT. ADYAR HEADQUARTERS-- HPB'S ROOM -- AFTERNOON

                    HPB
          So. What is it?

                    EMMA COULOMB
          I was told you are to meet the Maharajah again
          tomorrow. May I go with you?

                    HPB
          That is not appropriate. What business is it of yours
          to go there with me?

                    EMMA COULOMB
          Alexis and I are tired of being treated like peon in
          this place. Since you do not have any money, I want to
          ask the Maharajah to lend us 2000 rupees so we can get
          out of here and be on our own. You will be free of us,
          and we won't have to work like slaves.

                    HPB
          Slaves! We saved you. Remember? As for approaching
          the Maharajah, I have never heard of such! Impossible!
          You shall not dare show your face to him in front of
          me.

                    EMMA COULOMB
          If you do not let me go with you, you will regret it.

                    HPB
          How dare you threaten me! Under no circumstances will
          you go. Now, get out of here! Such insolence!

                    EMMA COULOMB
          You will never speak to me like a servant again,
          Madame. I will expose you as a fraud. You forget, I
          saved your life once. I knew you in Egypt. You will
          regret every word you have spilled on me today. You
          will see.

EXT. ADYAR HEADQUARTERS--HPB'S ROOM-- EVENING

We see a lone, flickering light from HPB's bedroom window.

INT. ADYAR HEADQUARTERS-- HPB'S ROOM -- EVENING

Olcott is sitting next to HPB's bed. She is out of breath and sick.

COLONEL OLCOTT
Dr. Dudley says you must change climates, otherwise you will be gone to this world in three months.

HPB
It is so hot. The Masters restored me in Darjeeling but here I can't breathe. The heat is killing me.

COLONEL OLCOTT
I'll accompany you to France. I have much I need to do in England and Germany. The problem with ANNA KINGSFORD in London is getting tense. I believe she thinks she can replace the venerable Helena P. Blavatsky. But the group around Sinnett won't let her. A power struggle.

HPB
Oh, Moloney. Both sides are at fault. Do they want power and fame or do they want to bear my cross? But the mere mention of that woman's name makes my head throb. Why the Masters insist on retaining her, I don't know. Yes, yes, do whatever needs to be done. I'm going to die soon wherever you put me. The old body is not good for much more.

COLONEL OLCOTT
Don't talk like that. You've only started the Secret Doctrine. That will keep you busy for years to come. Once we get you to Europe and a cooler climate, you'll feel better.

HPB
I don't have years, Moloney. Only months . . . I can feel myself fading out.

She falls asleep.

SOUND: Ringing of Tibetan prayer bowl

CUT TO:

INT. PARIS, FRANCE THEOSOPHICAL SOCIETY HQ -- MORNING

HPB is bundled in blankets and propped up in a comfortable armchair in the living room of her friend LADY CAITHNESS, the head of the Theosophical Branch in Paris and WILLIAM Q JUDGE, one of the original founders of the New York TS.

> LADY CAITHNESS
> Madame, a telegram from India arrived a few minutes ago.

> HPB
> Whatever could it be? Let me see it.

She rips open the telegram.

> TELEGRAM
> "Crisis at Adyar. Coulombs caught stealing money among other charges. Must fire them. Need your accord. Hartmann Board of Control"

> HPB
> My, my, now Emma's fury has been directed at TS. Before I left India I wouldn't lend her 2000 rupees. She tried to force her way to our Maharajah patron, and I wouldn't let her go. She's taking her vengeance out on me.

> LADY CAITHNESS
> This is your housekeeper in Adyar?

> HPB
> Yes, a complex story. She's a medium also. A bad one. Listens to any wicked voice that talks to her. Very dangerous in a sense. Yes, I must agree with the Board of Control to fire her. Duchess, could you send the following telegram through the PTT: "Sorry you must go. Prosper"

> WILLIAM Q. JUDGE
> Better be cautious with ex-employees. They can seek revenge in the most dastardly way.

> HPB
> Maybe it's a good thing I'm in Paris now.

> WILLIAM Q. JUDGE
> I don't know if you'll get the rest you need. There must be at least twenty persons who have solicited us to speak to you. What should I do?

> HPB
> Let them come and see this sick old lady. Master wants me to talk to them.

INT. PARIS THEOSOPHICAL SOCIETY HQ -- AFTERNOON

Two weeks later . . .

                    HPB
Damn! This can't be right! Judge, the Master asks me to try and guess what would be the most extraordinary thing he would order me to do right now.

                WILLIAM Q. JUDGE
That you should go to London and straighten out the turmoil in the London Lodge.

                    HPB
That's right.

                WILLIAM Q. JUDGE
Since Sinnett settled back in England and published his book on Esoteric Buddhism, I could sense there would be a conflict with Anna Kingsford's Hermetic bent.

                    HPB
Can't they see it all one and the same? Kingsford's a scourge to the movement and I cannot imagine why the Masters want to keep her. But we must obey.

                WILLIAM Q. JUDGE
So when are you going?

                    HPB
He's ordered me to take the 7:45 pm express from the Gare St. Lazare tonight! Can't he see I'm too sick and weak to travel?

                WILLIAM Q. JUDGE
What are you going to do?

                    HPB
Well, I must go even if I die on the train.

                WILLIAM Q. JUDGE
I'll accompany you.

                    HPB
No, I should go alone. You can continue working on the Secret Doctrine. From the pot into the coals, I say. The London Lodge seethes with conflict. I can feel it even in Paris. Will you take me to the station tonight?

                    WILLIAM Q. JUDGE
          Of course, Lady Caithness and I will see you to the
          station.

                                             CUT TO:

EXT. LONDON MEETING HALL -- EVENING

We see a couple enter the main door of the hall and follow them in.

                                             CUT TO:

INT. LONDON MEETING HALL -- EVENING

Fifty-plus people are sitting in a meeting hall to elect the new officers of the London Lodge of the Theosophical Society. Colonet Olcott is presiding. The air is charged.

                    COLONEL OLCOTT
          The results of the balloting are as follows: Mr.
          Finch, President. Mr. A.P. Sinnett, Vice-President and
          Secretary and Francesa Arundale, Treasurer.

There is a groan in the audience and roughly half the members begin to stand up. ANNA KINGFORD steps up to the podium.

                    ANNA KINGSFORD
          One moment, please. Let me say one more thing before I
          step down as President. This election has been
          weighted against me by the new officers who cannot see
          the relevance of our Hermetic traditions with the
          Buddhist. Many of us have no connection with India,
          but ALL of us have a connection with our Greek
          heritage. That this Society should . . .

Suddenly the main hall door in the back swings open and HPB walks in and takes a seat in the back row.

                    ANNA KINGSFORD (CONT'D)
          Show such prejudice to their own tradition in favour of
          one that is so alien to them is a farce. You are no
          more Buddhists than . . .

Suddenly, HPB jumps up from her seat and screams

                    HPB
          Mohini!

Mohini, the young Hindu whom HPB sponsored to go to Europe to study, jumps up from where he is seated in the front row and races down the aisle to where HPB is standing and throws himself down on the floor at HPB's feet. A.P. Sinnett jumps down off the podium and races down the aisle, then turns around to face the body

                    A.P. SINNETT
             (in a loud commanding voice)
      Let me introduce to the London Lodge--Madame Helena P. Blavatsky our leader and founder.

There are gasps and shouts from the audience. Some women break into tears and rush up to cluster around HPB.

                    HPB
      Please, please, my dear friends. Let us not get too emotional over this grouchy hippo. There are enough emotions in this hall tonight.

She walks up to the podium and manages a smile for Anna Kingsford who has remained there throughout the commotion.

                    HPB (CONT'D)
      I come not to take over your meeting but to offer a solution, one given me from the Master Kuthumi. He suggests that we create two lodges: One called the Hermetic Lodge led by our trusted friend, Anna Kingsford and the other the present London Lodge, led by the newly elected Mr. Finch. Colonel Olcott has already prepared the papers for the Hermetic Lodge.

There is a loud applause from the audience

                LONDON TS MALE MEMBER
      Why didn't we think of this simple solution?

                    HPB
      Because sometimes the simplest solutions are the most difficult to find in emotionally charged situation.

INT. MEETING HALL -- EVENING

Collage of scenes of HPB lecturing and meeting lines of people during her visit to London.

SOUND: Ringing of Tibetan prayer bowl leads us to Madras, India

                                CUT TO:

INT. MADRAS NEWSPAPER OFFICE -- DAY

Emma and Alexis Coulomb are plotting with Methodist REV. OLIVER in EDITOR JAKE SMITY on how to expose HPB.

                        EMMA COULOMB
I have everything here. Do you have your part, Reverend?

                        REV. OLIVER
Jake, give it to her.

Emma opens the envelope and counts out the 2000 rupees, and then gives the Reverend another envelope.

                        REV. OLIVER (CONT'D)
   (opening the envelope)
What have we here?

                        EMMA COULOMB
All of Madame Blavatsky's letters ordering Alexis and me to do certain things. Especially to build the shrine in her room.

                        REV. OLIVER
With . . .?

                        EMMA COULOMB
. . .with the trap door on the other side. All her so-called phenomena we would place in the shrine from the trap door in the adjoining room.

                        REV. OLIVER
You see, Jake. Here, we've got a solid case against this witch. This fraudster who works for the devil.

                        JAKE SMITY
How do we know she works for the devil?

                        REV. OLIVER
She's a magician. I've seen her at work. And only the devil would make such things happen. Ah, the Lord Jesus Christ is mixed with Buddha's and all those hideous Hindu gods. Damnation to them all.

                        EMMA COULOMB
A devil she is. We lived with her for years. I gave you all the inside information in the envelope, but if you want to interview us, that will be an extra 500 rupees.

                    REV. OLIVER
What do you say, Smity. An extra 500 rupees to get the
full story?

                    JAKE SMITY
          (shaking his head)
If God wills it and we can wipe out this scourge from
Madras, why not?

                    REV. OLIVER
Glory be the name of Jesus Christ whose honour and
truth we uphold! May India be ours again.

SOUND: Ringing of Tibetan prayer bowl leads us back to Europe.

                                        CUT TO:

EXT. GEBHARD HOME--GERMANY -- AFTERNOON

After her stay in London HPB seeks refuge in the home of GUSTAV AND
MARY GEBHARD in Elberfeld, Germany. Instead of rest, however,
there is a steady stream of visitors. MARY GEBHARD is at the front
door speaking to one of these visitors, FREDERIC MEYERS.

                    FREDERIC MEYERS
I just arrived this morning from London. I represent
the Society for Psychical Research. Mme. Blavatsky
knows me. We met two times while she was England. So
when I heard she was still in Europe, I rushed here to
see her. I have so many questions I wish to ask her.

                    MARY GEBHARD
She is quite sick and can't get out of bed today, but
she's consented to see you nonetheless. Please try not
to tax her.

                    FREDERIC MEYERS
I am very grateful. I will try not to tax her.

                    MARY GEBHARD
She said that if you wish to see any phenomena, I
should show you to the door.

                    FREDERIC MEYERS
Ah! This is understood. Thank you. May I see her
now?

INT. GEBHARD HOME --HPB'S BEDROOM -- AFTERNOON

HPB is propped up in her bed reading a book when Frederic Meyers walks in.

                    FREDERIC MEYERS
So sorry to bother you, Madame, but I rushed all the way from London to see you before you go back to India.

                    HPB
That was kind of you. But we've already met a couple times in England. Wasn't it with Mr. Oscar Wilde?

                    FREDERIC MEYERS
Yes, but this time I come in the name of the Society for Psychical Research which wanted me to interview you en profondeur, but I see you are not feeling well today.

                    HPB
The Masters have ordered me to consent to this interview. It is not my idea. So please proceed.

                    FREDERIC MEYERS
I'm very sorry . . . .

                                          FADE OUT:

INT. GEBHARD HOME --FOYER -- LATER

                    FREDERIC MEYERS
I'm afraid I may have exhausted her with questions. When she speaks of Theosophy, it's almost as if someone else takes over.

                    MARY GEBHARD
She's here to recuperate, yet how she works every day at writing her book!

                    FREDERIC MEYERS
I am to meet with her again tomorrow afternoon. This was her idea.

                    MARY GEBHARD
My, my, I shall never understand her. She can barely lift herself out of bed, yet she will never miss a good conversation on Theosophy.

                    FREDERIC MEYERS
          She is remarkable. It was just like that conversazione
          the London Branch held at Prince's Hall a few weeks
          ago--all the notables of London society, and though she
          was quite sick that day, she managed to hold her own
          that evening. With every meeting, my confidence in her
          teachings and who she is grows immeasurably.

                    MARY GEBHARD
          Well, I look forward to seeing you tomorrow.

Meyers leaves and Mary Gebhard closes the door.

INT. GEBHARD HOME--LIVING ROOM -- AFTERNOON

                    MARY GEBHARD
          Have you finished your writing for the day?

                    HPB
          Yes, the Masters left so much for me to do overnight
          that I could not rest this morning. Now it's time for
          some tea.

                    MARY GEBHARD
          It's all ready. By the way, you received this
          envelope, special delivery from Adyar via London this
          morning.

                    HPB
          I'm glad you did not give this to me in the morning.
          These kinds of envelopes always portend trouble.

HPB opens the envelope and pulls out newspaper clippings. One screams "The Collapse of Koot Houmi," another headline announces "The Fall of Madame Blavatsky: Her Intrigues and Deceits Uncovered." "Madame Blavatsky and her 'Himalayan Masters'Exposed as Frauds" She throws the envelope and contents down on the floor.

INSERT: Newspaper headlines from Madras screaming: "Inside Story on the fraudulent Madame Blavatsky?" "Domestic tells the Truth about Theosophical Society and its Founder" "A Hole in the Wall explains the so-called Phenomena of Blavatsky"

                    MARY GEBHARD
          What is wrong, Helena?

                    HPB
          It appears that Emma Coulomb, after being fired by the
          Board of Control, has allied herself with the Christian
          missionaries in Madras. They have published forged
          letters in the newspapers purported to be from myself
          to her.
                    (sobbing)
          I cannot take anymore of this! I am sick. The hostile
          winds are blowing on me. The whole world will turn
          against me and the Theosophical Society. Such vermin,
          these Coulombs! One step forward, ten steps backward.
          Expletives

                    MARY GEBHARD
          Who will believe them? You will see. There are too
          many people who love and respect you as the true
          emissary of the Trans-himalayan Brotherhood. No one
          will believe a housemaid.

                    HPB
          Look how the newspapers believe her. Don't they know
          she will lie just for a few rupees?

HPB begins to weep and swear at the same time.

                                                  FADE OUT:

INT. GEBHARD HOME--HPB'S BEDROOM -- AFTERNOON

The next day . . .

                    FREDERIC MEYERS
          No need to worry, Madame. Our Society for Psychical
          Research will set the record straight. We will send
          out our best, a young man you have already met.
          Richard Hodgson, a young teacher and graduate of
          Cambridge. He will undertake a scientific
          investigation of this whole situation and report back
          to the SPR.

                    HPB
          Please check first with Colonel Olcott. He will have
          the last say about this investigation. I myself am
          returning to India to prosecute these traducers of my
          character, these fabricators of letters.

                    FREDERIC MEYERS
          The SPR and I have full confidence in you, Madame.

> **HPB**
> Is your Society's reputation good enough to counter these lies, fabricated by those damn Christian missionaries and the Coulombs? I will prosecute them. May they burn in hell, all of them!
>
> **FREDERIC MEYERS**
> Please, Madame, don't excite yourself. We will surely take care of this situation for you . . . once and for all.
>
> **HPB**
> I must get out of this bed and go back to India immediately. I have my own plan.

SOUND: Hard ringing of Tibetan prayer bowl leads us to Port Said, Egypt

> CUT TO:

INT. PORT SAID ABOARD SHIP -- MORNING

HPB and a group from the London Theosophical Society--ISABEL COOPER-OAKLEY, her husband and a young Anglican cleric CW LEADBEATER-- gather together in HPB's cabin on the ship sailing back to India.

> **CW LEADBEATER**
> Ma'am. One of our fellow passengers just handed me this leaflet.
>
> **HPB**
> (glancing over the leaflet)
> Blatant lies. The missionaries continue their campaign against me even on board this ship. Charles, speak to the Captain about this and have him put a stop to this!
>
> **ISABEL COOPER-OAKLEY**
> I am ashamed of my own countrymen, HPB. How unfortunate, we must take the same ship with that whole band of missionaries Mme. Coulomb conspires with. Here are the documents my husband picked up for you at the police in Cairo.
>
> **HPB**
> These should be enough to prove these two conspirators are none other than blackmailers. I will drag them both back into the cesspools of Cairo along with the rest of those bible maniacs.

At that very moment, the Master Morya walks through the closed cabin door. Leadbeater is sitting on the floor gaping. The Master speaks confidentially to the group.

EXT. PORT OF MADRAS ARRIVAL -- MORNING

Ship bringing HPB, the Cooper-Oakleys, and Leadbeater arrives to a tumultuous welcome at pier, meant to be a public showing to counter the scandal the missionaries created in the Madras Newspapers.

INT. ADYAR TS HEADQUARTERS--COLONEL OLCOTT'S OFFICE -- MORNING

> HPB
> We gathered all the information on the Coulombs in Cairo. Cooper-Oakley got the police affidavit. The Coulombs skipped town in bankruptcy

> COLONEL OLCOTT
> But what has this to do with your particular case against them?

> HPB
> I will show the world they are but criminal elements of long-standing.

> COLONEL OLCOTT
> You have no case from these past witnesses. It's all hearsay. Just weather this storm, chum. It will pass.

> HPB
> You are all cowards when it comes to defending me. All of you!

> COLONEL OLCOTT
> But can't you see? Dragging this whole affair into the courts, you will also drag the Masters into the muck. Why would you want to do that?

> HPB
> Because we must defend ourselves on the level everyone understands in this world. In the courts. They have made a mockery of our work. All the hundreds of phenomena I produced are reduced to a hole in the wall. How could you cheapen our mission by giving into this scum?

> COLONEL OLCOTT
> The board and I agreed that the less said the better... just keep quiet and don't give them the pleasure of blowing this affair into a huge public scandal. Many members are dropping like flies from all our branches and the more this gets dragged into the public the more members we will lose.

> HPB
> Henry, can you not stand up for principle? This is like a dagger thrust into my heart, and your every word just twists it. Save your asses by letting my blood! You cowards! You will see how this matter will blow up in spite of your hiding.

> COLONEL OLCOTT
> I say, let this matter rest, Helena, or you will kill yourself. Besides, I must leave for Burma on tonight's ship for the International Buddhist movement.

HPB pounds her fist on Olcott's desk, gets up and stalks out of the office.

EXT. ADYAR TS HEADQUARTERS--ROOF VERANDA OUTSIDE HPB'S QUARTERS -- NIGHT

Months later in early 1885 COOPER-OAKLEY, DR. HARTMANN, BABULA, other members of the TS household keep a vigil outside HPB's room.

> ISABEL COOPER-OAKLEY
> Doctor says she may not live the night. This whole affair with the Coulombs has killed her spirit. But somehow, I'm certain she'll pull through. Her work is not done.

> DR. HARTMANN
> Just as a precaution, however, I sent your husband to Madras to secure a cremation permit.

> BABULA
> No, you will not need it. In this place many miracles have happened.

> ISABEL COOPER-OAKLEY
> Yes, Babula, we all think that way.

> DR. HARTMANN
> Damodor sent a telegram this afternoon to Colonel Olcott. He's in Burma. I asked him to come back as soon as possible.

                    ISABEL COOPER-OAKLEY
               Let's hope he gets back in time.

Suddenly they hear movement in HPB's room. They get up to check.

INT. ADYAR TS HEADQUARTERS--HPB'S QUARTERS -- NIGHT

HPB lies on her deathbed. She stirs. A tall transparent figure (barely outlining the Rajput Master) appears at her bedside.

                            MORYA
               Upasika. I have come in answer to your cries.

                            HPB
               Master, I am dying again. My body will not go on any
               longer. The mission is broken.

                            MORYA
               It need not be. You have a choice. Depart from this
               body and go in peace. Or remain in this body and take
               all the suffering it gives you until you finish The
               Secret Doctrine.

                            HPB
               I will finish my mission, sire. God willing, give me
               the strength to get out of this bed. My choice is
               made. I will work with you and Kuthumi to write that
               book. It must be done.

Morya smiles and touches HPB's crown and a wave of light streams through her body. She revives and slowly sits up. Morya disappears.

                       HPB (CONT'D)
               Isabel! Come!

Isabel Cooper-Oakley rushes in, followed by the others

                       HPB (CONT'D)
               Bring me some tea and some cakes. I'm hungry.

Babula kneels down next to HPB and weeps into her hand. Isabel kneels next to him weeping with joy.

INT. ADYAR TS HEADQUARTERS--A MEETING ROOM -- AFTERNOON

Around twenty people are gathered in a meeting called by A.O Hume at the TS headquarters

> A.O. HUME
> As a standing member of the Anglo-Indian Theosophical Society in Simla, I have traveled all the way from Simla to call this meeting. I wish to save this whole movement from utter disaster of the Coulomb scandal.

> MEMBER 1 IN AUDIENCE
> Many have already resigned but more have remained. We can weather this storm.

> MEMBER TWO FEMALE IN AUDIENCE
> I agree with Mr. Hume. Something must be done to rectify this terrible situation.

> MEMBER THREE IN AUDIENCE
> What do you propose?

> A.O. HUME
> The Coulomb revelations have clearly pinpointed that the present leadership of the society is comprised of frauds, something we have suspected for some time. There were never any Masters. Just fraudulent tricks. Why, the Coulombs should know, being so close to HPB.

He waves the Madras newspapers in the air.

> A.O. HUME (CONT'D)
> My proposal is simple. We must force Colonel Olcott, Mme. Blavatsky, Damodar, and the rest on this list of sixteen persons to resign immediately.

He waves a sheet of paper and gives it to a member to pass around the room.

> MEMBER 1 MALE IN AUDIENCE
> . . . If all these people resign, then there would be no one left to lead this society.

> A.O. HUME
> Precisely. We need new leadership. We can elect an interim group of officers who would dispose of this property and erect it elsewhere in India, perhaps even in Simla, a new Scientific-Philosophical-Humanitarian Theosophical body.

> MEMBER TWO FEMALE IN AUDIENCE
> The newspapers are full of lies. The Coulombs fed them with all their lies. She's just vengeful because Helena did not lend her some money.

> ISABEL COOPER-OAKLEY
> And how can you say the Masters do not exist? Some of us have been in their presence.

> MEMBER 1 MALE IN AUDIENCE
> With all due respects, your solution to save the society amounts to destroying it. We cannot act in this manner.

> MEMBER THREE MALE IN AUDIENCE
> I move we adjourn this meeting immediately, and that no further discussions of this nature be entertained ever again.

> ISABEL COOPER-OAKLEY
> (getting up to leave)
> I find it rather despicable that you would call this meeting while Mme. Blavatsky lies recovering from near death in bed upstairs and while Colonel Olcott is absent in Burma. Under her very nose, you are trying to undermine the very core of the society. Can't you see, it is their dedication and toil that built this society? If you're acting on principle then why don't you face the founders themselves with this proposal instead of undermining them behind their backs?

Everyone in the room stands up and exits leaving Mr. Hume alone at the podium.

INT. ADYAR TS HEADQUARTERS--HPB'S QUARTERS -- AFTERNOON

A few days later. Olcott rushes into the bedroom.

> COLONEL OLCOTT
> I got Damodor's telegram that you were dying when we arrived in Burma. I dropped everything and took the first boat back.

He takes HPB's hand and holds it.

> HPB
> I would have welcomed death at that hour. I so desired rest. The life that stared me in the face looked so miserable. Yet, how could I say no to Him who wanted me to live! Morya gave me an ultimatum. Finish the book or go in peace. Of course, it was never a choice. I have to finish the book.

COLONEL OLCOTT
But you look well, old chum. From what the others have told me, you were about to leave us.

HPB
Sorry you had to interrupt your trip, but I think I can carry on. The Boss restored my essence. It was those Coulombs. So full of lies. So many will abandon us because of them, bringing ill-repute on this precious society we worked so hard to build.

COLONEL OLCOTT
Let those who believe them go. Anyone in his right mind should see through those lies.

HPB
Then why don't you let me prosecute them. We must take action to clear my name and the Society's

COLONEL OLCOTT
I already told you I don't want to drag the Masters into a nasty court battle and make a great mockery of THEIR work?

HPB
What about the lies about me? We can't let them remain there. There must be a counterforce to them.

COLONEL OLCOTT
They will wither on the vine. We've already countered them in the newspapers. Our legal advisors are unanimous and took the decision during the annual meeting not to prosecute. So let it be.

HPB
Easy for you to say. Their attacks are levied at me. They will publish that report worldwide and make a mockery of the Society. How can you stand still and not do anything?

COLONEL OLCOTT
Is this our work to spend all our time fighting court battles? Legally it is a waste of time. In time all will be forgotten and the truth will shine through.

HPB
In the meantime, the world will step all over me. You are a traitor, Henry Steel Olcott. A traitor to the Cause. And you will be seen as such after I'm gone.

                    COLONEL OLCOTT
          I never thought I'd hear such words from you, Helena.
          You see how much I travel and work for the Cause?
          Every hour of my life is spent for this Society.

                    HPB
          Go back to Burma and your Buddhists! You were to bring
          occult truths to mankind, not run around creating
          branches for the sake of branches and associations for
          the sake of associations. These will all be dead
          shells in a generation, but an occult truth gently laid
          upon mankind will permeate all branches of knowledge
          and carry mankind forward. That's more than I can say
          for these crystallized organizations you are so fond of
          creating! Go back to Burma and stay there!

Olcott gets up and leaves HPB's bedroom. He slams the door behind him.

INT. ADYAR TS HEADQUARTERS--COLONEL OLCOTT'S OFFICE -- DAY

The next day . . .

                    COLONEL OLCOTT
          HPB is not herself.

                    MARY SCHARLIEB MD
          The Coulomb scandal has really taken a toll on her. It
          has had a devastating effect on her emotions despite
          the numerous interventions of the Masters.

                    COLONEL OLCOTT
          And of course the heat here in Madras. In a couple
          months it will be like a furnace here.

                    MARY SCHARLIEB MD
          She will not last long in this heat. This combined
          with all the agitation surrounding Mr. Hume's attempt
          to destroy the society, I thought we would lose her for
          sure then.

                    COLONEL OLCOTT
          Yes, behind my back too! Maybe we should send her back
          to Europe. Would that do her some good?

                    MARY SCHARLIEB MD
          I would say so.

COLONEL OLCOTT
We should start a subscription right away to help defray her medical costs and send her to Europe then to live. With her gouty fingers, weak heart, and albuninaria, I doubt if she will ever be able to do much henceforth.

MARY SCHARLIEB MD
She is still determined to finish her work, no matter what.

COLONEL OLCOTT
We must regard her as our pensioner, and see that she is kindly cared for. Poor woman. After slaving so hard for the world, that she should be driven away from home to die with a stigma of disgrace fastened upon her brilliant name.

MARY SCHARLIEB MD
Then we must get her out of Madras. Perhaps she will find peace of mind in Europe.

EXT. PORT OF MADRAS -- DAY

March 31, 1885 . . .

A crowd gathers to see HPB off at the port. HPB is carried on a sedan chair by 8 porters. She is accompanied by Mary Flynn, Bawaji (Hindu chela) and Dr. Hartmann. Olcott stands stiffly among them as HPB is lowered to the ground.

HPB
My work will continue in spite of you, Moloney.

COLONEL OLCOTT
I can only hope so.

HPB
Never would I have thought that you would exile me in such a way.

COLONEL OLCOTT
It is for your health.

HPB
Look at me straight in my eyes and repeat that. You, my only chum in the world, are lying to me. You can't wait to get rid of me so I won't embarrass your precious Society any longer. Go ahead, dare to look at me.

HPB weeps uncontrollably. Olcott lowers his head. The ship's crew call for last boarding.

> COLONEL OLCOTT
> You are my chum to my dying day. You must know that. You must board now. I will come to see you in Europe. I promise you. We will make sure you are taken care of.

The porters struggle to lift HPB's sedan chair, then march her up the gangplank. Tears stream down HPB's face as she is carried away. She does not even acknowledge the good-byes from the group on the pier. There's a finality in the good-byes. That HPB will never return is reflected in the faces of her well-wishers.

SOUND: Using the wooden baton to rub the lip of the Tibetan prayer bowl creates a mournful ringing.

> CUT TO:

INT. HPB'S APARTMENT WURZBURG, GERMANY -- MORNING

Fall of 1885

> COUNTESS WACHMEISTER
> I was just about to leave for my vacation in Italy when I received your telegram telling me to come.

> HPB
> Well, my dear Countess Wachmeister. This is surely not the grand palaces and noble mansions that you are used to.

> COUNTESS WACHMEISTER
> When I saw you last year in London, you mentioned that I would eventually devote my life to Theosophy. I thought that strange and improbable. But the way things have turned out in my life, here I am. Yes, my dear friend, if I can help, let me stay with you.

> HPB
> At first I told you not to come because I have very little space here to accommodate you. But Master told me that I should ask you again to come. All I have is this sitting room, a small kitchen and bathroom and that small bedroom with two beds. At least it is warm and dry in here. And I get wonderful light from this window, even as it gets cold outside.

                    COUNTESS WACHMEISTER
          With my husband gone and the children grown, I see life
          differently. If you need my help, then I am willing to
          stay. We can put up a screen between the two beds and
          it will be like two small bedrooms!

                    HPB
          Your presence will be a blessing beyond words!

INT. HPB'S APARTMENT WURZBURG -- NIGHT

Pages of handwritten text drift down from the ceiling onto HPB's writing desk and settle into a stack. An invisible hand works on HPB's finished drafts, and one can see notations being written in the columns with blue or red ink.

INT. HPB'S APARTMENT WURZBURG -- MORNING

As usual HPB's desk is stacked with papers. She is sitting as usual in her big chair at her desk staring into space when the Countess walks in and hands her a large envelope.

                    HPB
          There is very bad news inside.

                    COUNTESS WACHMEISTER
          It's too early in the morning to fret about this, HPB.
          Here, take a cup of tea first.

                    HPB
          I know, the SPR released their report on me last month.
          Olcott sent this copy to me. It will read like
          fiction. I can already see the copies of these letters
          I supposedly wrote to Emma. Outright lies. How can
          that young man Hodgson be so evil? He was supposed to
          tell the truth about the Coulombs but instead turns on
          me. He's says I'm a Russian spy.

INSERT: Society for Psychical Research in England Upholds Allegations: "Mme. Blavatsky denounced as a Russian Spy and Occult Fraud."

                    COUNTESS WACHMEISTER
          This is a scoundrel, who deserves none of your
          attention.

HPB
And his superior, Meyers. That bastard. I let him question me for three hours while I was bedridden last year. He was convinced that the Masters were true to life. He promised me that the SPR would set everything straight. Now, look what they've done! They've joined the ranks of my detractors. BAH! The SPR can go to hell. One day after they've killed me with their lies, the truth will ring through.

COUNTESS WACHMEISTER
Conspirators of the lowest order, at best.

HPB
Countess, go, please go before you are defiled by my shame. You cannot stop here with a ruined woman who will be pointed at every where as a trickster and impostor.

COUNTESS WASCHMEISTER
I listen to my heart, Helena, not to news reports.

HPB
One thing is a consolation; the whole burden falls upon me in this report, because the Masters are made out as myths. Hodgson says I made them up to trick people. So much the better. Their names have been desecrated too long and too much by human ignorance.

COUNTESS WACHMEISTER
My husband held many high positions and the higher he got, the more enemies he encountered. The more known you get, the more they attack you.

HPB
It's the hurt done to the Theosophical Society. I can already see mass resignations from bright lights in the society and I see over the horizon insulting letters coming from men and women who have worn the mask of friendship. The rest of the members will remain paralyzed and will want to hide from the ridicule of their friends. Alas, so few will stand up for me or principle. So few, even among those who witnessed phenomena and even have in their possession the "gifts of the Masters" will turn against me.

COUNTESS WACHMEISTER
One thing I learned from being the silent witness of my husband's travails, dear friend, is that time seems to wash away these acts of evil and betrayal. They create

a momentary sensation, but in due time even their audience tires of them.

                HPB
You are right. I shall lie low. I'm here today only because I promised the Masters that I would finish this book.

                FADE OUT:

SOUND: Quick taps on Tibetan prayer bowl lead us back to Wursburg, Germany

                CUT TO:

INT. HPB'S APARTMENT WURZBURG -- NIGHT

More pages of handwritten text drift down from the ceiling onto HPB's writing desk and settle into a stack. Other similar stacks of paper are on the table. A small lamp on the desk turns itself off once the stack has been completed.

INT. WURZBURG HPB'S APARTMENT -- NEXT MORNING

            COUNTESS WACHMEISTER
The Masters have piled more work on your desk. You must get to work again. I wish I could help you.

                HPB
You don't know how much your presence is a comfort. You cannot imagine what it is to feel so many malicious thoughts and currents directed against me; it is like the prickings of a thousand needles, and I must continually erect a wall of protection around me.

            COUNTESS WACHMEISTER
Who's sending you these unfriendly thoughts?

                HPB
I am always trying to shut my eyes so as not to see and know. I can see certain people writing these horrible letters. Here, these two I received this morning. I already know what's in them. Isabel wrote to tell me that Mr. Hume went to Adyar and tried to get the Council to force me and Olcott to resign, because we are frauds.

            COUNTESS WACHMEISTER
Here's a letter from Mr. Judge. This should cheer you up. He's never given in to all this gossip.

HPB
AH, William Q. He was one of the original founding members of the TS, you know, in New York. Let me see that.

HPB scans the letter and smiles.

HPB (CONT'D)
This is one out of a hundred. But I wonder about Olcott. Has he abandoned me, too, as night closes in on our creation?

COUNTESS WACHMEISTER
He still works diligently on the copies of your manuscript I send him every week. No, I'm sure he'll never abandon you. The Theosophical Society is your love-child.

HPB
I can't work with all this tumult around me.

COUNTESS WACHMEISTER
I have an idea. Let's go to the seashore. The fresh air and change of landscape should revive you. I have in mind a place in Ostend, on the North Sea coast of Belgium.

CUT TO:

INT. OSTEND, BELGIUM SUITE OF ROOMS -- EVENING

A group has gathered outside HPB's room. She is again on her deathbed.

COUNTESS WACHMEISTER
Mary, thank you so much for coming.

MARY GEBHARD
I dropped everything and came. How is she?

COUNTESS WACHMEISTER
She lost consciousness while writing two days ago. The doctor said there is a serious malfunction of her kidneys. He says it's hopeless. She will pass any time now.

MARY GEBHARD
She has pulled through similar crises.

> COUNTESS WACHMEISTER
> I telegraphed Dr. Ellis in London. He's arriving tomorrow. It's good to get another opinion. She is sleeping quietly but the scent of death lingers in her bedroom. I will stay with her tonight any way.

INT. OSTEND SUITE OF ROOMS-- HPB'S BEDROOM --NEXT MORNING

> HPB
> Countess, wake up!

> COUNTESS WACHMEISTER
> Helena! Why you're supposed to be . . .

> HPB
> Dead?

> COUNTESS WACHMEISTER
> Why yes, I mean . . . the doctor said you weren't expected to make it through the night.

> HPB
> Master came last night. He again gave me choice: die and take the easy way out or go on with the work at the risk of facing even greater difficulties than ever. So, I'm back. I'm hungry. I'm ready for breakfast.

> COUNTESS WACHMEISTER
> (beaming)
> Well, HPB, you look well. In a few days I guess we'll be ready to leave for London. The KEIGHTLEY brothers from the London Lodge came while you were sick and packed up everything. Your manuscript is safely put in that truck so you can get to it easily.

> HPB
> Give me a couple more days near the sea and I'll be ready to go. Ah! Every time I come out of these near death experiences, I feel renewed and all the controversy and evil that swirl around me seem inconsequential.

SOUND: Quick taps on Tibetan prayer bowl lead us back to England.

INT. MAYCOT, ENGLAND HOME -- DAY

Little cottage with stacks of papers and boxes surrounding HPB's writing desk and chair. HPB in the midst of the papers is working as usual at her writing desk when Dr. BERTRAM KEIGHTLEY and his brother ARCHIBALD, members of the London Branch of the Theosophical Society, enter.

                    DR BERTRAM KEIGHTLEY
Well, still working, I see.

                    HPB
Master dropped more text last night and I'm trying to integrate them. There's more of the manuscript over there.

HPB points to a stack of papers about three feet high.

                    ARCHIBALD KEIGHTLEY
A monumental work, probably the occult work of the century! But . . .

                    DR BERTRAM KEIGHTLEY
. . . the way the text reads so far will confuse many a reader, especially those who are not familiar with the occult. It's without plan, structure, or arrangement.

                    ARCHIBALD KEIGHTLEY
We'll continue working with Colonel Olcott to give it more structure and organize the text in a logical fashion.

                    HPB
You both have my blessings. Do whatever you need to do. Move the text around and organize it better with Olcott. He's very good at structuring things. Make it ready for the publisher. But do not change a word.

                    DR BERTRAM KEIGHTLEY
We'd never be that presumptuous.

                    HPB
The countess has sent more of the manuscript to Olcott and he will want to put his two cents in for sure.

                    DR BERTRAM KEIGHTLEY
Then the transit time of the mail between England and India will add to the time we spend preparing it for the publisher.

                    HPB
How long do you think you will need?

DR BERTRAM KEIGHTLEY
From experience, it may take a year or slightly less. Look at that stack! I've never worked on anything so monumental.

HPB
Take it, my friends. It's all yours.

FADE OUT:

INT. MAYCOT ENGLAND HOME -- MORNING

Several months later . . .

HPB is writing at her desk. Suddenly someone bangs on the front door and HPB's housekeeper LOUISE runs to the door. Bertram Keightley rushes in. He is carrying the thick manuscript.

DR BERTRAM KEIGHTLEY
Mme. Blavatsky, here is the manuscript of the Secret Doctrine which we had to have typed before handing it to the printer.

HPB
Hummm. Give it here. Looks much neater than my chicken scratch.

DR BERTRAM KEIGHTLEY
But, Madame, there is a serious problem.

HPB
What's that?

DR BERTRAM KEIGHTLEY
The entire volumes III and IV are missing. Didn't you say there were four volumes? I swear you showed me those two sections months ago, but they're gone. Disappeared.

HPB
(smiling wryly)
Yes.

DR BERTRAM KEIGHTLEY
You even refer to them in your introductory remarks.

HPB
(still smiling))
Yes.

> DR BERTRAM KEIGHTLEY
> Then, where are they?

> HPB
> Master ordered me to pull them out at the last minute. After the Maha Chohan reviewed humanity's reception of Theosophical teachings, it was decided that it would take another fifty to a hundred more years before that information could be released to humanity.

> DR BERTRAM KEIGHTLEY
> Then it was premature?

> HPB
> Can't you see by the opposition and vicious attacks I've had to endure up to now? Look at the way our own Theosophical Society members have been lapping up the Hodgson Report. They prefer lies to the Truth. Humanity is too anchored in materialism and that information would serve no purpose.

> DR BERTRAM KEIGHTLEY
> Then it will not be released within our lifetimes.

> HPB
> No. Another messenger will appear in the Twentieth Century to bring that information to humanity.

> DR BERTRAM KEIGHTLEY
> Well, then. I'll just have to wait until I reincarnate to read those pearls of wisdom.

> HPB
> (laughing)
> Perhaps you won't have to wait that long. Why not read them between incarnations! I'll be up there too, to show you the two volumes.

>> FADE OUT:

INT. MAYCOT, ENGLAND HOME -- EVENING

A large group has squeezed into HPB's tiny cottage. They are sitting on the desk, floor, and chair arms. HPB sits in her wheelchair. They are a younger set (30's and 40's) Among them is MOHANDAS GANDHI.

HPB
Occult phenomena failed to produce the desired effect. It was supposed that intelligent people, especially men of science, would at least have recognized the existence of a new and deeply interesting field of inquiry and research when they witnessed physical effects produced at will which could not be explained scientifically. Even theologians misunderstood and misrepresented them. Phenomena did excite curiosity in the minds who witnessed them, but these minds were of the idle type. The greater number of the witnesses developed an insatiable appetite for phenomena without any thought of studying the philosophy or science behind them.

MOHANDAS GANDHI
Did that science behind the phenomena have anything to do with Hinduism?

HPB
Yes. And the same goes for Esoteric Buddhism and Christianity. That science pervades all these religions and understanding it gives you the answers to phenomena.

MOHANDAS GANDHI
Surely there are Hindu yogis today who can produce such.

HPB
Yes, indeed. But I think they too, have come to the same conclusion as we did: An occultist or yogi can produce phenomena, but he cannot supply the world with brains!

The listeners chuckle.

HPB (CONT'D)
What is needed is the intelligence and good faith necessary to understand and appreciate them.

MOHANDAS GANDHI
Understood, Madame.

HPB
Young man, one of these days you shall play a major role in the liberation of your country.

                    MOHANDAS GANDHI
That I should have such grand ambitions would shock me
at this moment. I'm almost penniless.

                    HPB
You will see. Now, group, let me propose that we
organize a new publication, something along the lines
of the Theosophist. . . . The main reason being the
difficulty in trying to edit the Theosophist in India
from here.

                    LISTENER 1
Would it compete with the Theosophist?

                    HPB
That is not my purpose. It should complement it. I
would like to call it Lucifer.

The whole room stirs.

                    LISTENER 2
But why, Madame? Why name it after the fallen
Archangel Lucifer?

                    HPB
Ah, my friend, that's where you are mistaken. The
original meaning of Lucifer is the Light-Bringer.
Lucis means "light." Ferre means "to carry". Christ
Jesus was a Lucifer. It's only because of Milton's
Paradise Lost that Lucifer has become synonymous with
fallen angels and spirits.

                    LISTENER 1
How would this magazine be different?

                    HPB
Our articles would be so thought-provoking as to
hopefully break the apathy settling into our Society.
The Theosophical Society is not a social club, as most
people think. It is a carrier of light that provokes
change in human thinking in preparation for the great
changes on earth that will come about during the next
century. We must begin to break down the staid,
church-like social and dogmatic veneer and prepare each
person to be a temple unto himself.

                    LISTENER 2
Hear! Hear!

INT. LANSDOWNE ROAD, LONDON -- EVENING

Fall-Winter 1888. . .

HPB has been moved to more spacious quarters as the number of visitors wanting to meet her personally increased since the publication of the Secret Doctrine.

INSERT: Shots of visitors in and out of her quarters, classes with 20 to 30 people surrounding her writing desk. HPB is sitting her wheelchair.

INT. LANSDOWNE ROAD, LONDON -- DAY

SUMMER, 1889 . . .

Enter ANNIE BESANT, HPB's successor in the Theosophical Society

> HPB
> My dear Mrs. Besant. I have so long wished to see you. The review you did for the publisher of the Secret Doctrine did justice to my work. It showed a deep understanding that I could only wish my best students in theosophy would grasp.

> ANNIE BESANT
> The Secret Doctrine is a monumental work which revolutionized my thinking. I am no longer the woman I was before I read it.

> HPB
> My dear Mrs. Besant, if you would only come among us!

> ANNIE BESANT
> This is my greatest desire.
>   (kneeling before HPB)
> Will you accept me as a pupil and give me the honour of proclaiming you as my teacher before the world?

> HPB
> You are a noble woman. May Master bless you.

INT. LANSDOWNE ROAD, LONDON -- NIGHT

September, 1889 HPB sits in her wheelchair opposite Olcott, a desk in between them in HPB's Landsdowne room. As usual the desk is piled with papers.

> HPB

Well, Moloney. Just like old times in New York. Here, while you're sitting here, help me correct these proofs of "A Key to Theosophy." So many around us do not understand what we're teaching, so I thought this work would clarify some of our concepts.

          COLONEL OLCOTT

It's been a long time, chum. I've missed you tremendously in Adyar.

          HPB

I had to go through these past years alone, although the Masters always surrounded me with friends who took care of me. The heat in India would have killed me and the Brotherhood would never have gotten the Secret Doctrine out of me!

          COLONEL OLCOTT

As you know, I, have not spent much time in Adyar as I've been traveling quite a bit. I also had my share of problems. A group of our members staged a coup and wanted to have me replaced by a committee. They said I was too dictatorial.

          HPB

What? After all you have done to build up Adyar?

          COLONEL OLCOTT

Yes. I was quite unhappy. I went to Japan last month. They want us to unite all the disparate elements of Buddhists around the world together. What an opportunity to do what we were sent here to do! They wanted me to head the Buddhist religion in Japan. I figured if our own society was plotting aginst me, I could be of more use the Buddhists in Japan. But Morya wouldn't allow it and the coup did not succeed.

          HPB

Look at me, chum. I'm in no physical shape to head any organization and the Masters know that. So you'd better stay with it. They were supposed to release me after the Secret Doctrine was published and I was ready to go. I'm here today only because they want me to start the Esoteric Section of the TS. I have a couple more things I must do before I exit.

          COLONEL OLCOTT

Our work will never end, but there will come a time when we have to retire. Come back to India with me, ole chum.

                    HBB
The heat will kill me instantly.

                    COLONEL OLCOTT
I checked with the doctor. He said if you live in a
cool place it should be alright. Listen, I've
purchased a small property up in the western Ghats in
Ootacamund. You've been there. It's beautiful and
cool there all year round and sunny, too. I thought we
would both retire there in Mother India.

                    HPB
          (tears in her eyes)
Henry, my days are numbered and I think you know that,
too. I have chosen my successor. Her name is Annie
Besant. Keep your eye on her, and if she is the person
I think she is, then let her take my place.

                    COLONEL OLCOTT
          (taking her hand)
It hurts to hear you speak like that, but all missions
must come to a close. You were right. I was making
too much out of the organization. But your work here
in Europe has now served to balance our work. We now
have a solid organization that is growing throughout
the world with the Secret Doctrine as the underpinning
of all its teachings.

                    HPB
My place is here to complete the last details of this
incarnation. But Ah, Ootacamund! If I had the
strength and health. . . I remember those exquisite
rose gardens, the breathtaking views, and the coolness.

          (she squeezes Olcott's hand)

But no. I can't. My last ounce of energy must be
devoted to consolidating the Esoteric Section and
finishing this last book.

                    COLONEL OLCOTT
I understand, old chum. By the way, I officially
chartered the Esoteric Section. I know deep down that
I shall have to carry on after you. You kept us both
on track.
          (He kisses her hand)

                    HPB
You're leaving tonight?

                    COLONEL OLCOTT
          Yes, by the boat train and then to Marseilles to catch
          the ship back to Madras.

He stands up and walks around HPB's desk, leans over her and
embraces her for a long time.

                    HPB
          Henry, I don't know if I'll ever see you again but I
          want you to know this: I love you more than anyone on
          earth save Master. My friendship and BROTHERLY
          affection for you are eternal. My dear chum, carry on
          our mission. Don't let it die.

SOUND: Ringing of Tibetan prayer bowl giving in and out vibrations.
(This is achieved by holding bowl on palm and moving it in a
circular motion while tapping bowl).

                                        CUT TO:

INT. SIDNEY, AUSTRALIA LECTURE HALL -- EVENING

Several months later on May 9, 1891 Olcott is lecturing on
Theosophy to a crowded hall, standing room only

                    COLONEL OLCOTT
          . . . one of the principles of Theosophy as reiterated
          so clearly in Mme. Blavatsky's recent work "The Voice
          of the Silence" . . .

Olcott stops in the middle of his sentence as if listening to an
internal voice

                    HPB (V.O.)
          . . . my dear chum, I have departed.

He pauses for a moment, gritting his teeth as tears well up in his
eyes. He takes out his handkerchief and wipes his eyes, swallows
hard then continues speaking.

                    COLONEL OLCOTT
          . . . is that it is based on the Tibetan Book of the
          Golden Precepts and is said to represent the highest
          state of Buddhism, Mahayana Buddhism, in a form
          understandable to the western mind.

NARRATOR
Helena P. Blavatsky expired on May 8, 1891, but through her works she has lived on to challenge every succeeding generation. Her monumental works Isis Unveiled, The Secret Doctrine, the Voice of the Silence and the Key to Theosophy underpin the whole non-church spiritual movement that pervades our world today. Many of their precepts and principles so shocked 19th Century thinkers, but today stand embedded and taken for granted in modern spiritual thinking. These works continue to challenge human thinking. In 1986, one hundred years after its publication, the Society for Psychial Research issued an apology to Mme. Blavatsky stating that the Hodgson Report had unjustly condemned her.

www.ingramcontent.com/pod-product-compliance
Lightning Source LLC
Chambersburg PA
CBHW080511110426
42742CB00017B/3077